漢 語 初 階

（上）

BEGINNING STANDARD CHINESE

by

Helen T. Lin

Chinese Department
Wellesley College

Part I

(Revised 1990)

華語教學出版社　北京

SINOLINGUA BEIJING

First Edition   1 9 9 2
Second Printing   1 9 9 6

ISBN 7—80052—116—8
Copyright 1992 by Sinolingua
Published by Sinolingua
24 Baiwanzhuang Road, Beijing 100037, China
Printed by Beijing Foreign Languages Printing House
Distributed by China International
Book Trading Corporation
35 Chegongzhuang Xilu, P. O. Box 399
Beijing 100044, China

Printed in the People's Republic of China

PREFACE

Shortly after completing the manuscript of this book, our mother, Helen T. Lin, learned that she was terminally ill with cancer. Throughout her remaining five months, preparing for this book's publication was uppermost in her mind. She viewed this as the culmination of a life's work, embodying the pedagogical philosophy that underlay a successful teaching career. Before she died, she instructed her daughters to convey this view to her readers.

Our mother was emphatic that language learning should be a way of discovering new worlds. And, it should be fun. This requires language teaching to be stimulating and the classroom a place of intellectual rapport for both the teacher and the student. Our mother wanted the student's command of Chinese to be not only a bridge between cultures, and an instrument of peace, but also a source of creative self-expression.

But our mother was also one to demand immediate results. So, she wanted a textbook that would teach students to build rapidly a large repertoire of useful expressions from the limited material taught to first-year students. She drew on her twenty years of teaching experience to guide her choice of that minimal set of characters and sentence structures that would yield the optimal result. Chinese being a living and rapidly evolving language, there were always new challenges to be met. Not knowing that her health was failing, meeting these challenges often drained her. During those times, she would remark that this book had caused her to burn her candles from both ends.

The original material she wrote was tested in that very best living crucible called the Wellesley College Chinese Department. For two years, mother's most stern and supportive critics, her colleagues from the Department tried this material on their own students and brought back comments and suggestions from their classroom encounters. Together with Theresa Yao, Bing Shaw, Ruby Lam, William Liu, and Michael Crook, much of the original text was revised, improved. Mother repeatedly expressed her appreciation and affection for them. She considered the years spent with them and Marya Maung of the Chinese Department among the most enriching in her life.

If she could preface this book herself, mother told us, she would use the occasion to express her love and deep gratitude for her husband, Andrew Lin, for his unwavering confidence in her, through this and many of her other projects.

She would have also wanted to acknowledge the support from Chen Xiaoming, Zhou Kuijie, Ni Jia and the staff from the Foreign Languages Press in Beijing. Sensitive to her belief that the only viable language textbook is a current one, they, in consultation with Theresa Yao and Ruby Lam, undertook to update the vocabulary and expressions that have developed over the last two years. Thus, in the best spirit of international collaboration, a new life has been breathed into our mother's work by those she most loved and respected.

Catherine and Vivian Lin
1988

TABLE OF CONTENTS

INTRODUCTION

For most students, the primary objectives in studying a foreign language are to acquire proficiency in doing research in original materials, and to have direct meaningful contact with the people of the country he or she is studying. This is why a good solid foundation is most important. However, in view of the rapid social, economic, and political changes in Taiwan and Mainland China in the recent three decades and the associated impacts on the language, and in view of the increasing desire of American people to acquire a more substantive understanding of New China, an up-to-date, non-intensive, first-year (class meeting about 5 hours per week) textbook for college students is badly needed. Such are the reasons for the publication of *Beginning Standard Chinese* and the student's workbook.

Putonghua, or the standard Chinese is the chief dialect of the Han (漢) people who constitute the majority of the 1.1 billion population in China. It is the declared Chinese national language on both sides of the Taiwan Straits. Although it is a language spoken by the greatest number of people, Chinese is more frequently characterized as a language with a long history and distinctive attributes. This set of teaching materials provides the students with about 610 characters—forming a core vocabulary most prevalently found in PRC and Taiwan, among which, about 530 characters are chosen for active knowledge and are to be reproduced from memory by students. These characters provide approximately 1,150 vocabulary expressions covered in the lessons. All the basic sentence structures in spoken Chinese are introduced in a rather systematic and scientific way. The book, *Essential Grammar for Modern Chinese*, written by the author (Boston: Cheng and Tsui Company, Inc., 1981), can be used as a compendium for further analysis and explanation of Chinese grammar. Teachers and students are strongly advised to use it as a main reference when using *Beginning Standard Chinese* as their text. The purpose of this book, on the other hand, is to emphasize a balanced language training: to develop the student's abilities in speaking, listening, reading, writing and translating simultaneously.

The material included in the textbook as well as in the student's workbook is presented in romanization version along with Chinese characters in both regular and simplified forms, thus, these books are not designed to be taught by just the oral-aural teaching method. The *pinyin* romanization is used as an expeditious medium to introduce pronunciation. How to make a student's pronunciation and intonation resemble as closely as possible that of a native speaker is a keen issue in language teaching. Hence, the sound practice is not just a mainstay in the first lesson, but also is an important part of every lesson through the whole text. The vocabulary and structure included in this series have been selected mainly based on the following materials, and you will quickly notice my heavy debt to these scholars:

Speak Mandarin Text by Henry C. Fenn and M. Gardner Tewksbury, New Haven: Yale University Press, 1967.

Speak Mandarin Student's Workbook by Henry C. Fenn et. al., New Haven: Yale University Press, 1967.

Introduction to Chinese Pronunciation and the Pinyin Romanization by Hugh M. Stimson, New Haven: Far Eastern Publications, Yale University, 1975.

Spoken Standard Chinese Vol. I by Parker Huang and Hugh M. Stimson, New Haven: Far Eastern Publications, Yale University, 1976.

Beginning Chinese revised edition by John DeFrances, New Haven: Yale University Press, 1976.

Elementary Chinese 2 vols. by Beijing Language Institute, Beijing: The Commercial Press, Part 1, 1971; Part 2, 1972.

Elementary Chinese Readers Vol. 1 and 2 by Beijing Language Institute, Beijing: The Foreign Languages Press, 1980.

Practical Chinese Reader Vol. 1 and 2 by Beijing Language Institute, Beijing: The Commercial Press, 1981.

and two language survey papers conducted and written by the author, the first one was done in Taiwan and the second was done in PRC:

"Survey of Commonly Used Expressions in China and an Analysis of Its Possible Implication on Language Teaching on the College Level," published by ERIC of the Center for Applied Linguistics, 1974.

"A Survey of Common Expressions Used in Daily Life in the People's Republic of China" published by ERIC of the Center for Applied Linguistics, 1982.

The objective of the first lesson of the textbook and workbook is the introduction to the Chinese pronunciation and practice. Each of the ensuing lessons builds upon given key Chinese grammatical points (sentence structure) with selected vocabulary.

Each lesson of the textbook contains the following:

1. A text which can be either a short story, dialogue, a letter, or in other forms, first written in *pinyin* romanization and then followed by Chinese character version in both regular and simplified forms.

2. The new vocabulary, ranging from daily life to student activities, is listed with part of speech and Chinese characters in regular form and in simplified version if it applies, then, the English equivalent (s) can be found at the end of each entry.

3. A list of about 20 or more characters chosen from current and previous lesson(s), for students to reproduce from memory.

4. The introduction and explanation of new sentence patterns.

5. Grammar notes and others.

6. English translation of the text.

In the student's workbook, written jointly by Helen T. Lin, Theresa C-H Yao and Bing Shaw, the first lesson focuses on pronunciation and intonation drills, plus some useful expressions from daily life and classroom activities. It also demonstrates how to write some very simple and basic Chinese characters. Starting from lesson 2, each lesson contains the following:

1. Vocabulary drills.

2. Pattern drills.

3. An introduction to writing new required characters with a practice sheet provided.

4. Questions made based on the text.

5. Exercises such as pyramid drill, situation games, and grammar exercises.

6. Translation from English into Chinese.

7.　Other supplementary reading material, which is optional.

In some lessons, you may also find Yao's computer games and/or exercises for further consolidation of the knowledge of vocabulary or grammar.

The text, vocabulary, sentence patterns in the textbook of each lesson as well as the pronunciation drills, vocabulary drills, pattern drills and supplementary readings in the *Student's Workbook* should be recorded. Before attending class, the student should review the teaching material with the recording, until he can say them all fluently, and if possible, from memory, so that in class he may participate in drills without referring to the books. As a result, the student will be able to listen and understand the work, grasp the grammatical concepts and develop his speaking ability before establishing reading and writing proficiency.

In terms of reading and writing, neither the regular nor the simplified characters will be neglected. This is because, while over 2,300 popular characters were simplified by PRC and adopted in this form as official in 1957, the simplified form is banned in Taiwan. Knowing both forms of characters will enable the student to be able to read and learn about the current situation not only in Taiwan and Mainland China, but also in all other overseas Chinese communities as well. However, it is extremely difficult for a beginner to master both forms simultaneously. This book suggests that, although you should be able to recognize both forms, an attempt should be made first to reproduce the regular form from memory, and progress on to both forms after one semester of training.

Before embarking on the main task, it seems helpful to know some important characteristics of modern Chinese, especially in the areas of speech sound, character, words and grammar.

1.　Speech Sound: Each square-shaped Chinese character contains one syllable made up of three elements; (1) an initial consonant(s), (2) a final vowel(s) or vowel-consonant(s), and (3) a tone. These may be regarded as characterizing the whole syllable. As a result of sound-simplification over many centuries, the spoken standard Chinese, as typified by speakers from the city of Beijing, has only just over 400 basic monosyllables. Even though such stressed syllables may contain four different tones regularly, and sometimes a neutral tone, the total sound-resource of standard Chinese is approximately in the range of 1600-2000 separate items. Compared with other Chinese dialects, such as the Wu dialect, Amoy, Cantonese, and the European language as well, *Putonghua* (standard Chinese) shows a paucity of sounds.

2.　Characters (zì 字) and Words (cí 詞): The Chinese language has no alphabet. Each syllable appears as a character in writing. The written form of the Chinese characters remains the same throughout the country and is shared by speakers of all other national dialects. Today, *Putonghua* is the national language, and its pronunciation is not only 'standard' among all Han people, but is also the principal means of communication among China's more than 50 minority nationalities.

Ancient Chinese writing is usually described as being pictorial or ideographic. Chinese characters are traditionally classified into six categories called *liushu*; (1) the pictographs, (2) ideographs, (3) compound ideograms, (4) loan characters, (5) phonetic compounds, and (6) derivative characters. Phonetic compounds comprise by far the majority of all characters. Since the ancient times, the pictographs or ideographs have disappeared as the written characters have become closely associated with the words of the spoken language.

The total number of Chinese characters is estimated at more than 50,000 (there are about 47,021 to be found in the *Kang Xi* (*Kang Shi*) *Dictionary*, which was compiled in the Qing Dynasty and is considered the most complete), however, only about 5,000-8,000 of them are commonly used, and of these, about 3,000 are used mainly for everyday purposes. The characters have been arranged according to their component parts, and are categorized by 214 radicals. This system is the one most widely adopted by the Chinese dictionaries using regular characters. When the simplified character form was officially adopted by the PRC government in 1957, the number of radicals was reduced to 189, and alphabetical order has also been adopted for compiling new dictionaries since then.

A Chinese character always has one syllable, and as such, is considered a "free" word, but not all Chinese words are necessarily monosyllabic words. When we analyze the structure of Chinese sentences, we find that the smallest distinctive and complete units of meaning (cí 詞) are often combinations of two or more syllables. Such basic semantic units, whether of one or more syllables, are more like the words in other languages. From what has been said above, it is clear that, in Chinese, a word may be represented by one, two or more characters, but not every character can singularly form a unit with a distinct meaning. In fact, a few dissyllabic words are such that the first character of the word is never found away from the second. Most importantly, a Chinese word, be it monosyllabic or polysyllabic in sound, bound or free in form, cannot have its meaning discerned out of context. You should be aware that the meaning of each word may undergo a substantical change in meaning as it is used in different syntactical structures. Thus, a command of Chinese syntax is essential in learning Chinese.

3.   Some Basic Concepts in Chinese Grammar: The Chinese grammar contains some key differences from the grammar of English familiar to most students — particularly in the following ways:

(A)   A word can assume different functions when it is placed in different positions in sentences. Furthermore, unlike English, there is no '-ing,' '-ly' or '-tion' to indicate the part of speech for a given word. An expression will 'look' the same whether it is used as a noun or a verb.

(B)   Number is not indicated by attaching suffixes to nouns or verbs, but by using a construction of "number-measure" which precedes the noun.

(C)   Chinese personal pronouns do not vary in form in the nominative,   possessive or objective cases.

(D)   Chinese verbs are not conjugated. The tenses are usually shown by the time expression or by various verb suffixes indicating the different aspects.

Therefore, an effective way to study Chinese, especially spoken Chinese, is to first learn the parts of speech of each expression while studying the new vocabulary, then inserting the vocabulary into the appropriate position in sentences, which can be formed according to the various prescribed patterns of sentence structure.

The definition and function of each kind of the parts of speech can be found in the grammar notes of the lesson when they first appear. For a more systematic and complete explanation, please check Helen Lin's book, *Essential Grammar for Modern Chinese*, Chapter II, Words and Parts of Speech.

The symbols in the following table occur in this text as the abbreviations of parts of speech.

Table of the Symbols for the Parts of Speech

		First Appeared Lesson
A	adverb	2
AV	auxiliary verb	3
BF	bound form	4
CV	coverb (prepositional)	5
Conn.	connective	9
DO	direct object	3
EV	equative verb	2
EX	expression	2
FV	functive verb	2
I	interjection	5
IO	indirect object	3
IV	intransitive verb	2
L	localizer	9
M	measure word	4
MA	movable adverb (conjunction)	2
N	noun	2
NU	number	4
O	object	2
P	particle	2
PN	personal pronoun	2
PW	place word	9
PV	post verb	5
QW	question word (interrogative pronoun)	2
RV	resultative (compound) verb	16
RVE	resultative verb ending	16
S	subject	2
SP	specifier (demonstrative pronoun)	4
SV	stative verb (adjective)	2
T	(prestated) topic	4
TS	time-spent	13
TV	transitive verb	2
TW	time-word (or expression)	7
V	verb	2
VO	verb-object	2

Lesson 1

Introduction to Chinese Pronunciation: Sounds and Intonation and Basic Strokes in Chinese Characters

Most Chinese people find it difficult to begin learning their language with traditional orthographic methods, thus, in recent decades, both Mainland China and Taiwan have adopted a phonetic system as a medium to teach preschool children to learn Chinese. The phonetic system prevailing in Taiwan is the National Phonetic System which uses 37 phonetic symbols, beginning with ㄅ, ㄆ, ㄇ, ㄈ, while Mainland China uses *pinyin* with the Roman alphabet. Obviously, it is less of a burden on an English-speaking student to learn Chinese language with romanized phonetic systems. Currently, the *pinyin* romanization is most widely used in American schools, as well as the mass media.

I. SOUNDS

As we know, a Chinese sound generally can be divided into three parts: (1) an initial, which is the first part of a sound, (2) a final, that is a vowel(s) or vowel + consonant(s) cluster following the initial consonant(s), and (3) a tone. In modern Chinese, there are altogether 21 initials and 38 finals. An initial usually is one consonant, such as: **b, d, g, x, c, q, z**..., or a cluster of two consonants, such as **zh, ch, sh**.... A final may contain just one vowel as in: **a, e, i, o, u, ü**, or a two—vowel cluster, as in: **ai, ao, ei, ou**, and a cluster of one vowel followed by the consonant **n** or consonant **ng**, as in: **an, en, in, un, ang, eng, ong**...; and occasionally -r can be found as the last letter in a syllable indicating a retroflex ending, as in: **-ngr** or **-anr**. The vowels **i, ü** and **u** can also be used as semi-vowels to form the finals: **ia, iao, ie, iong, ua, uo, uang, ue**, etc. However, compared with English, the sound system in Chinese is much simpler, for Chinese has a much smaller inventory of vowels and consonants.

A. Initials: The symbols of 21 initials used in *pinyin* romanization are as follows:

Table I Initials

Mode of Articulation / Point of Articulation	Stops		Affricates		Nasals	Lateral	Spirants	
	Unaspirate	Aspirate	Unaspirate	Aspirate	Voiced	Voiced	Voiceless	Voiced
Bilabial	b-	p-			m-			
Labiodental							f-	
Tongue tip-alveolar	d-	t-					h-	
Tongue dorsum-soft palate			j-	q-			x-	
Tongue tip-hard palate			zh-	ch-			sh-	r-
Tongue tip-upper teeth			z-	c-			s-	

In addition, a Chinese syllable may begin with a vowel such as: a-, e- or o-; or with a semi-vowel i, ü or u. At that time, the consonants y and w are used instead. No one can find two languages having exactly the same speech sounds. You should try to discover in what way you have to modify the pronunciation pattern of your own language so that your faults in the new language pronunciation can possibly be reduced. The following initials have a sound value in Chinese similar to that in English:

The Unaspirated and Aspirated Stops: b-, d-, g-, and p-, t-, k-: The initial sounds b-, d-, and g- are unaspirated. They do not have a strong puff of breath; and the vocal cords are not vibrating, which means they are not voiced.

      b like the p in spp, not like the b in bay

      d like the t in stay, not like the d in die

      g like the k in skate, not like the g in guy

The initial sounds p-, t-, and k- are aspirated as in English, but with a stronger puff of air, so:

      p like the p in pie

      t like the t in tie

      k like the k in kite

but they all have a much stronger aspiration than their English counterparts.

The Hissing Sound, a Spirant: h-: The initial h- is one of the voiceless continuants in Chi-

2

nese, called a spirant. When one is producing a spirant, the air from the lungs is constricted in the mouth tightly enough to produce a hissing sound, but not tightly enough to stop the passage of air completely. The Chinese h- is much rougher than the English h-. It is more or less like the ch in the German word na<u>ch</u>, since the Chinese h- is produced with the tongue in the same position as for g- and k-, but with a hissing sound.

Tongue Blade-Hard Palate Affricates and Spirants; j-, q- and x-: The initial j- is produced by first raising the front of the tongue to the hard palate and pressing the tip of the tongue against the back of the lower teeth, then loosening the tongue to let the air squeeze out through the channel between the tongue and hard palate. The vocal cords do not vibrate in pronouncing this sound. The difference between producing j- and q- is that the latter one is aspirated. J- and q- are affricates, somewhat like the initials of English <u>j</u>eer and <u>ch</u>eer, <u>ch</u>eap. The x- sound, a voiceless spirant, is produced by raising the front of the tongue to, but not touching, the hard palate, leaving a narrow opening through which the air escapes causing audible friction and with no vibration. The Chinese x- is somewhat like <u>s</u>ee in English, but with the jaw moving downwards a bit.

Retroflex Affricates and Spirants; zh-, ch-, sh- and r-: This group of initials is made with the tip of the tongue. During their production, the tongue tip is drawn back to a position slightly behind the alveolar ridge, allowing a narrow opening between the tongue tip and the hard palate for the air to squeeze out. Zh- and ch- are voiceless affricates, which means that there are two audible phases in their pronunciation. A stop phase is first, followed by a spirant phase. However, zh- is unaspirated, while sh- is aspirated. Sh- is a voiceless spirant. They are rougher than the English counterparts since the tip is curled far back. The initial r- is a voiced spirant pronounced in the same way as sh-, but with vibration. The Chinese r- is not like the English r-; neither does it have the Scottish burr nor the French gutteral sound. It is not a trill.

Tongue-Tip and Hard Palate Affricates and Spirant; z-, c- and s-: The initials z- and c- are affricates produced by first pressing the tip of the tongue against the back of the upper teeth, then lowering it to let the air squeeze out through the narrow opening; the vocal cords do not vibrate. Z- is unaspirated while c- is aspirated. This unaspirated and aspirated pair consisting of z- (or "dz" in the Yale system), and c- (or "ts-" in Yale) does not occur is English in the initial syllable position. One may look for sounds similar to them between words, as in:

dad's high	it's high
it's Al	it's Hal

The initial s- is a spirant which means it is a hissing sound. This initial is relatively easy for an English speaker to produce since s- is like the initial of the English word sun.

The group of initials zh-, ch-, sh-, r- joins the initials z-, c-, s- in being used as complete syllables--that is, without a recognizable vowel after them. Whatever sound there may be is represented by the letter i, which is the representative letter of the blade-palatal vowel i, giving the syllables: zhi, chi, shi and ri, and zi, ci, and si; but the vowel i never comes after those initials in common speech in Chinese, so it must not be pronounced as i.

B. Finals: There are 6 vowel letters in the Chinese phonetic alphabet: a, e, i, o, u and ü. The Chinese vowels are not like English vowels which have more than one value. Therefore, it is important to determine which of the values given to a certain letter in English correspond to spoken Chinese.

The Group of Single Vowels:

a	as in father
e	as in her, but after y- as in yet.
i	as in machine
o	as in worm
u	as in rule, but with more lip-rounding and with the tongue drawn farther back
ü	This sound does not exist in English, but is common to both German and French. It is like the German ü in über, and the French u in rue. The Chinese ü is produced by pursing one's lips as if to say oo of ooze, then, with the lips in that position, try to say ee as in beet instead.

A Cluster of Two Vowels:

ai	as in aisle
ao	like the au's in sauerkraut
ei	as in eight
ou	as in boulder

A Cluster of Vowel and Consonant(s):

an	between o in con and a in an, but closer to o
ang	like a in father plus ng in song
en	like un in under
eng	like ung in lung
er	like er in her: er is a retroflex final which can stand for a syllable all by itself. Sometimes er is attached to another final to form a retroflex final which is transcribed by adding the letter r to the original final, e.g., wanr (to play), huar (painting). However, one can find fewer expressions with this retroflex final in standard Chinese than in Beijing dialect.
in	as in pin
ing	as in sing
ong	roughly, u as in put plus ng as in sing
un	seems like wen in Owen
ün	somewhat as in the French word une.

Finals with Semi-Vowel i: Since the finals in this group can also stand for a syllable by themselves, i

4

should be changed into the initial y-. For example, **ya, yao, ye,** etc.

ia	like the **ya** in **ya**cht
iao	like the **yow** in **yow**l
ie	like the **ye** in **ye**t
iu	in the first and second tones, close to **u** in **u**nion; in the third and fourth tones, close to **yo** in **yo**ke
ian	like the **i** in mach**i**ne plus a sound between the **an** of m**an** and **en** of m**en**
iang	like **i** in mach**i**ne plus **a** as in f**a**ther plus **ng** as in si**ng**
iong	like **i** in mach**i**ne plus a Chinese **ong** sound

Finals with Semi-Vowel **u**: When the final stands for a syllable by itself, **u** should be replaced by an initial **w**, e. g. , **wa, wu, wai,** etc.

ua	like the **wa** in **wa**nder
uo	like the **wa** in **wa**ter
uai	like **wh**y
ui	like **wei** in **wei**gh; as a syllable alone, the spelling is **wei**
uan	starts with a **w** sound, then ends like the Chinese **an**
uang	starts with **w**, then ends like **ang**
ueng	starts with **w**, then ends like **eng**

Finals with Semi-Vowel **u**: In this group, when a final stands for a syllable by itself, **ü** should be replaced by **yu**, such as **yue, yuan, yun,** etc. Moreover, the symbol **ü** is used only when the final is preceded by the initials **l** and **n**. If it follows other initials, like **j-, q-, x-.**, etc. , the symbol **u** is used instead of **ü**.

üe	**ü** is like the French **u** in r**u**e, plus e as in y**e**t
üan	**ü** the same as above, plus **an**

The final -i: This is represented by the symbol [ι] to show the initial which precedes it can stand for a syllable all by itself, as: **zi, ci, si, zhi, chi, shi** and **ri**. This i must not be pronounced. The above mentioned 37 finals plus **e** (as in **ye**) make all the 38 finals in the Chinese language.

C. Tone: As we know, a Chinese syllable of sound is made up of three elements. Besides initials and finals, tone is also a key factor in presenting a Chinese sound with a particular meaning. The tone is a variation of pitch, mainly that of its height, rising and falling. It has no relation to the intensity of sound. The tone rises and falls by gliding, not bounding. Except for certain interjections, every syllable in Chinese has its definite tone. A Chinese word or syllable that conveys a certain meaning when pronounced with a certain tone will yield either a different meaning or no meaning at all if pronounced with a wrong tone. The meaning of each of the following examples is obviously affected by varying the tone:

mā 媽   mother

5

má 蔴		hemp
mǎ 馬		horse
mà 罵		curse
ma 嗎		an interrogative particle

Standard Chinese has four tones. Each tone has its own characteristic pitch contour or set of contours. If the average range of the speaker's voice is divided into four equal intervals separated by five points, the four tones can be diagrammed as follows:

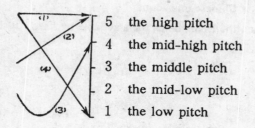

5	the high pitch
4	the mid-high pitch
3	the middle pitch
2	the mid-low pitch
1	the low pitch

The first tone is called a "high level tone" with pitch 55, and it uses - as its tone mark. The second tone is a high rising tone with pitch 35, and the tone mark is ´. It is also called a "rising tone." The third tone is called "low tone." It is a "falling and rising" tone. The sound descends from the mid-low pitch to the low pitch and then rises up to the mid-high pitch. In other words, the tone travels within pitch 214. The tone mark is ˘. The fourth tone is a falling tone with pitch 51, and its tone mark is `, so it is called "falling tone." The tone marks are put over the top of a vowel or, in the case of compound vowels, over the vowel that is pronounced loudest and longest e. g. , **shàng, xiǎng, xiāo, yuè** and **cái**. The four tones are different in length, the third tone being the longest and the fourth one the shortest, but with stress on the initial.

In addition to the four tones, there is a tone which occurs on stressless syllables and has a pitch entirely determined by the tones of adjacent syllables. This tone is called a neutral tone. If a neutral tone comes at the end of an utterance, it is affected by the tone of the preceding syllable. A neutral tone is unmarked. The easiest way to produce a neutral tone is by stressing the tone of the preceding syllable according to its characteristic. For instance, in the expression **tāde** (his), one may prolong the **ā** sound and keep it on a high level. In the expression **háizi** (child), one should make **ái** even higher than for an ordinary rising tone. For **jiǎozi** (Chinese meat dumpling), one should stress **ǎo**, and make it even lower than usual. For the fourth tone, such as in **zhèige** (this one), the sound of the initial **zh** is much stronger than it would be in the original fourth tone, so the speaker may make his voice drop down sharply. If a neutral tone stands at the beginning of an utterance, it is pronounced at about the midrange of the speaker's voice.

If two or more third tone syllables are spoken in uninterrupted succession, only the last remains as a third tone; the preceding one(s) should be changed to a rising tone.

More information about tone changes can be found in the grammar notes for the respective lessons.

II. INTONATION AND STRESS

A.   Intonation Pattern: The Chinese language is often described as exhibiting a melody-like pattern. This is because of the four tones that one hears. The melody in the Chinese language, roughly, is relatively short and rapid, but sharply up and down, and the voice is lower at the end of the sentence. There are four intonation patterns in Chinese regarding the mood of the sentence.

1.   Descriptive Mood - It is rather flat from the beginning to the end of a sentence. Only the adverbial expression is slightly stressed.

2.   Imperative Mood - One starts the sentence with a heavier sound and makes it even heavier toward the end.

3.   Interrogative Mood - It starts almost the same way as the descriptive sentence, but stress is put on the question word and the voice is raised at the very end of the sentence in order to form the voice of a question.

4.   Exclamatory Mood - This follows almost the same pattern as descriptive sentences, but the range is much wider than that of the descriptive pattern.

B.   Stress: Generally speaking there are three degrees of stress for polysyllabic words in spoken Chinese that can be distinguished: strong stress, medium stress and weak stress. The stress can be distinctly differentiated in the pronunciation of an expression of many syllables. An expression with two, three, or four syllables has a distinctly strong stress falls on the second syllables, and the first syllable is usually pronounced with a medium stress. For instance, in expressions such as **zàijiàn** (goodbye), **xuéxiào** (school), **hǎokàn** (good looking), etc., the second syllables are heavier than the first. A small number of disyllabic words, however, have the main stress falling on the first syllables, and the second syllables are usually pronounced with weak stress, e. g. , **wǒmen** (we, us), **péngyou** (friend), **shénme** (what), etc. Moreover, when a word is formed of reduplicated characters, the first syllable receives a strong stress and the second one is pronounced in the neutral tone, e. g. , **māma** (mother), **bàba** (father), **kànkan** (take a look), **xiǎngxiang** (think it over).

In a series of more than two syllables, normally, the last syllable is loudest, the first syllable is less loud, and any intervening syllables are least loud, but still louder than a syllable carrying the weak stress. The only reliable method for establishing good intonation rhythm is prolonged exposure and repeated practice.

1. Please read and try to remember the following list of expressions for some class activities:

    a. Zǎo!   Good morning!

    b. Nǐ hǎo a?   How are you?

    c. Hǎo! Xièxie.   Fine! Thank you.

    d. Shàng kè le.   It is time for class.

    e. Qǐng kàn shū.   Please read your books.

    f. Qǐng bié kàn shū.   Please don't look at your book.

    g. Qǐng nǐ niàn.   Please read.

    h. Qǐng nǐ dà shēng niàn.   Please read loudly.

    i. Qǐng nǐ zài niàn yi biàn.   Please read it again.

    j. Qǐng zài shuō yi cì.   Please say it again.

    k. Dàjiā yíkuàir niàn.   All of you read together.

    l. Dàjiā gēn wǒ niàn.   All of you read after me.

    m. Wǒ niàn, nǐmen tīng.   I'll read, and you will listen.

    n. Wǒ shuō, nǐmen xiě.   I'll speak, and you will write it down.

    o. Wǒ wèn, nǐmen huídá.   I'll ask and you'll answer.

    p. Yǒu wèntí ma?   Do you have any questions?

    q. Yǒu. /Méiyǒu.   Yes, I have. /No, I don't have any.

    r. Nǐ dǒngle ma?   Do you understand?

    s. Dǒngle. /Bùdǒng.   I understand. /I don't understand.

    t. Hǎo, xià kè le, zàijiàn!   All right, class is over, goodbye!

    u. Zàijiàn, lǎoshī!   Goodbye, teacher!

2. Here is a Chinese classical poem. You may find it interesting and would like to read it aloud. Please try to feel the intonation and the rhythm:

静 夜 思

床前明月光，

疑是地上霜，

舉頭望明月，

低頭思故鄉。

JÌNG   YÈ   SĪ

(In the Quiet Night)

Written by Li Bai (701-762 in the Tang Dynasty)

Chuáng qián míng yuè guāng.

Yí shì dìshang shuāng.

Jǔ tóu wàng míng yuè.

Dī tóu sī gùxiāng.

Translation:

So bright a gleam on the foot of my bed.

Could there have been a frost already?

Lifting myself to look, I found that it was moonlight.

Sinking back again, I thought suddenly of home.

III.   COMPONENTS OF CHINESE CHARACTERS

Chinese characters, the written symbols of the Chinese language, are, in general, constituted of several parts. Each part of a Chinese character is called a "component" of the Chinese character. The arrangement of the components in a character is either side by side or one above another, or else some components are also characters when they stand by themselves. The components of Chinese characters are composed of a number of basic strokes. Most of the characters are made of two components, either side by side or one above the other, one a semantic component which indicates the meaning, and the other a phonetic component which indicates the sound. (As pronunciation has changed over the centuries, however, many phonetics now indicate only the approximate sounds or none at all.) The following are the ten most basic strokes in forming all Chinese components, or one can say, that they form all Chinese characters. Students are strongly urged to practice them in order to lay a solid foundation in learning Chinese. The ten basic strokes are:

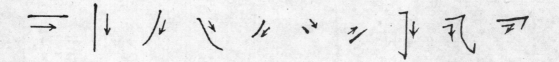

From these strokes, one can see that there is a general direction for writing each stroke. A few of the main principles are:

1.   Horizontal lines are written from left to right.

2.   Vertical lines are written from top to bottom.

3. Slanted lines of the form   are written from upper right to lower left.

4. Slanted lines of the form   are usually written from top left to lower right.

There is a great difference between handwritten characters and the printed style. Sometimes the disparity is so great that it is difficult to recognize two characters as the same. People should realize, however, that this can occur in almost every language.

A List of Numbers from One to Ten for You to Reproduce from Memory:

一	yī	(one)		六	liù	(six)
二	èr	(two)		七	qī	(seven)
三	sān	(three)		八	bā	(eight)
四	sì	(four)		九	jiǔ	(nine)
五	wǔ	(five)		十	shí	(ten)

NOTE

Most examples on pronunciation are taken from the following books:

John DeFrancis, *Beginning Chinese*, second revised edition. New Haven, Conn. : Yale University Press, 1976.

Hugh M. Stimson, *Introduction on Chinese Pronunciation and the Pinyin Romanization*. New Haven, Conn. : Far Eastern Publications, Yale University, 1975.

——————— *Introduction to Chinese Pronunciation*. New Haven, Conn. : Far Eastern Publications, Yale University, 1972.

Lesson 2

Functive, Equative and Stative Sentences

PART I. TEXT

Dialogue: **Shū Hǎokàn**——Books Are Interesting

I. *Pinyin* Romanization:

Xuésheng: Zǎo! Wǒ shì xuésheng, wǒ xìng Gāo. Nín guì xìng?

Lǎoshī: Zǎo! Wǒ xìng Wáng. Wǒ shì lǎoshī. Nǐ jiào shénme míngzi?

Xuésheng: Wǒ jiào Gāo Guì.

Lǎoshī: Gāo Guì, nǐ hǎo ma? Nǐ kàn shénme ne?

Xuésheng: Hǎo! Wǒ kàn shū ne.

Lǎoshī: Shū hǎokàn ma?

Xuésheng: Shū hǎokàn.

Lǎoshī: Shū guì buguì?

Xuésheng: Shū guì, kěshi shū hǎokàn. Bào búguì, kěshi bào bù hǎokàn.

Lǎoshī: Tā shì shéi? Shì bushì xuésheng?

Xuésheng: Tā yě shì xuésheng. Tā hěn gāo, yě hěn hǎokàn.

Lǎoshī: Nǐmen máng bumáng?

Xuésheng: Wǒmen hěn máng.

Lǎoshī: Nǐmen lèi ma?

Xuésheng: Wǒmen bú lèi, nín ne?

Lǎoshī: Wǒ hěn máng, yě hěn lèi.

Xuésheng: Zàijiàn, Wáng lǎoshī.

Lǎoshī: Zàijiàn!

書 好 看

學生： 早！我是學生，我姓高。您貴姓？

老師： 早！我姓王。我是老師。你叫什麼名字？

學生： 我叫高貴。

老師： 高貴，你好嗎？你看什麼呢？

學生： 好！我看書呢。

老師： 書好看嗎？

學生： 書好看。

老師： 書貴不貴？

學生： 書貴，可是書好看。報不貴，可是報不好看。

老師： 她是誰？是不是學生？

學生： 她也是學生。她很高，也很好看。

老師： 你們忙不忙？

學生： 我們很忙。

老師： 你們累嗎？

學生： 我們不累，您呢？

老師： 我很忙，也很累。

學生： 再見，王老師。

老師： 再見！

书好看

学生： 早！我是学生，我姓高。您贵姓？

老师： 早！我姓王。我是老师。你叫什么名字？

学生： 我叫高贵。

老师： 高贵，你好吗？你看什么呢？

学生： 好！我看书呢。

老师： 书好看吗？

学生： 书好看。

老师： 书贵不贵？

学生： 书贵，可是书好看。报不贵，可是报不好看。

老师： 她是谁？是不是学生？

学生： 她也是学生。她很高，也很好看。

老师： 你们忙不忙？

学生： 我们很忙。

老师： 你们累吗？

学生： 我们不累，您呢？

老师： 我很忙，也很累。

学生： 再见，王老师。

老师： 再见！

PART II. VOCABULARY——SHĒNGCÍ 生詞

PRONOUNS (PN):

13

我		wǒ	I, me
你		nǐ	you (singular)
您		nín	you (singular form used in polite speech)
他		tā	he, him
她		tā	she, her
我們	我们	wǒmen	we, us
你們	你们	nǐmen	you (plural)
他們	他们	tāmen	they, them (refers to males, or with mixed sexes)
她們	她们	tāmen	they, them (refers to females)

NOUNS(N)：

學生	学生	xuésheng	student
老師	老师	lǎoshī	teacher (lit., old master)
名字		míngzi	name, given name
書	书	shū	book
報	报	bào	newspaper

INTERROGATIVE PRONOUNS(QW)：

誰	谁	shéi(shuí)	who, whom
什麽	什么	shénmen	what

ADVERBS (A)：

也		yě	also

Tā xìng Gāo, wǒ yě xìng Gāo.

他姓高，我也姓高。

(His family name is Gao,
my family name is also Gao.)

Wǒ kànshū, yě kànbào.

我看書，也看報。

(I read books, and also newspapers.)

很	hěn	very, quite; very much
不	bù-, bú-, bu-	not

Tā bù gāo.

他不高。

(He is not tall.)

Nǐ kàn bukàn shū?

你看不看書？

(Do you read books?)

MOVABLE ADVERB (MA):

可是	kěshì	but

Wǒ bùmáng, kěshi hěn lèi.

我不忙，可是很累。

(I'm not busy, but I'm tired.)

EQUATIVE VERB (EV):

是	shì	be (am, are, is, was, were, etc.)

Tā shì xuésheng.

她是學生。

(She is a student.)

FUNCTIVE VERBS (FV):

姓	xìng	surname;　have a surname
叫	jiào	to be called;　have a given

15

			name
			Nǐ jiào shénme míngzi?
			你叫什麼名字?
			(What is your name?)
			Wǒ jiào tā lǎoshī.
			我叫他老師。
			(I call him teacher.)
看		kàn	to read, to look, look at
			Shéi búkàn shū?
			誰不看書?
			(Who doesn't read books?)

STATIVE VERBS (SV):

高		gāo	be tall
貴	贵	guì	be expensive; be honorable
			Shū bú guì.
			書不貴。
			(The book(s) is/are not expensive.)
好		hǎo	be good
			Nín hǎo a!
			您好啊!
			(How do you do?)
忙		máng	be busy
累		lèi	be tired, be exhausted
			Nǐmen lèi bulèi?
			你們累不累?
			(Are you tired or not? Are you tired?)
好看		hǎokàn	be interesting; good-looking
			Bào bù hǎokàn.
			報不好看。

〔The newspaper is boring
(not interesting).〕

PARTICLES (P): (see pattern)

嗎	吗	ma	(interrogative particle used to form simple questions)
啊		a	(semi-interrogative particle used in greetings)
呢		ne	(ending particle used to form an abbreviated question)

Tāmen máng, nǐ ne?

他們忙，你呢？

(They are busy! And you?)

EXPRESSIONS (EX):

早		zǎo	Good morning!
貴姓	贵姓	guìxìng	Your surname please? (Lit., your honorable surname)
再見		zàijiàn	Goodbye (lit., see you again)

SOME CHINESE SURNAMES:

高		Gāo
王		Wáng
林		Lín
姚		Yáo
柯		Kē
劉	刘	Liú
馬	马	Mǎ
宋		Sòng

司馬　　司马　　Sīmǎ

PART III. A LIST OF CHARACTERS REQUIRED
TO BE REPRODUCED FROM MEMORY

我 你 他 她 您 們 書 報 誰 什 麼 很 也 不 是 可
姓 叫 看 早 高 好 忙 累 貴 嗎 呢

PART IV.　SENTENCE PATTERNS

2. 1.　Simple Stative Sentence： In a stative sentence, the main verb, which forms the predicate of the sentence, is a comment on the nature, status or condition of the sentence subject. The subject of this sentence takes no action at all. The verbs used in this structure are "to be" plus adjectives, such as "to be tall," "to be good," etc., and they are called stative verbs (SV) (see note) in Chinese grammar. All stative verbs can have another preceding adverb as a modifier. So a simple sentence structure can be drawn as："Subject—Adverb—Stative Verb" to make a complete topic, which is the subject, and comment, which is the predicate.

	Subject	Predicate
	(Topic)	(Comment)

Pattern： S　　　(A)　　　SV.

Ex　1： Wǒmen bú lèi.
我們不累。
(We are not tired.)

Ex　2： Shū hěn guì.
書很貴。
(The book(s) is/are very expensive.)

Ex　3： Bào bù hǎokàn.
報不好看。
[The newspaper is boring (not interesting).]

18

2. 2. **Equative Sentence with Shì 是**：   The function of this type of sentence is to indicate whether two things are equal or not. In Chinese, the verb **shì** links two nouns, and forms the structure："Noun A (not) Equal Noun B"，and so **shì** is called an equative verb (EV) (see note). The nearest English equivalent to the Chinese **shì** is the copula "to be." **Shì 是** is used only in sentences with substantive predicates.

Pattern： N1 (bu) EV N2.

    Ex 1： Tā **shì** lǎoshī.

             她是老師。

             (She is a teacher.)

    Ex 2： Wǒ bú**shì** xuésheng.

             我不是學生。

             (I'm not a student.)

    Ex 3： Tā bú**shì** xuésheng, wǒ yě bú**shì** xuésheng.

             他不是學生，我也不是學生。

             (He isn't a student, I'm not a student either.)

2. 3. **Simple Functive Sentence**：   The functive sentences use those verbs to show actions of their subjects. The verbs which explain actions are called functive verbs (FV) (see note). A simple functive sentence may consist of three main parts："Subject—Functive Verb—Object." Functive verbs can be modified by an adverb which is placed before them, but can not be modified by placing the adverb **hěn 很** immediately before them in a sentence. The negative modifier **bù 不** can be inserted immediately in front of a functive verb to deny that the subject is engaged in the action specified by the verb.

Pattern： S (A) FV O.

    Ex 1： Tāmen bú kàn shū.

             他們不看書。

             (They do not read books.)

    Ex 2： Wǒ jiào Gāo Guì.

             我叫高貴。

             (I am called Gao Gui. My name is Gao Gui.)

2. 4. **Three Types of Questions**：

    A.   Simple question with the interrogative particles (P) (see note)：

1. It is very easy to make a simple question by just adding **ma** (嗎) at the end of a statement, such as **Tāmen máng ma?** 他們忙嗎? (Are they busy?).

Pattern 1: <u>S (A) (A) SV P?</u>

      Ex: Tā bù gāo ma?

         她不高嗎?

         (Is she not tall?)

Pattern 2: <u>S (A) (A) FV O P?</u>

      Ex: Tā bú kàn shū ma?

         她不看書嗎?

         (Doesn't she read books?)

2. The particle **ne** 呢 represents an abbreviated question with a specific point, such as: **Wǒ hěn lèi, nín ne?** (I'm very tired, are you?). The particle **ne** in this case replaces the predicate or the sentence object in the second clause to form a new interrogative sentence:

Pattern 1: <u>S1 SV, S2 ne?</u>

      Ex: Shū guì, bào ne?

         書貴,報呢?

         (Books are expensive. How about newspapers?)

Pattern 2: <u>S1 EV/FV O, S2 ne?</u>

      Ex: Tā bú kàn bào, nǐ ne?

         她不看報,你呢?

         (She doesn't read newspapers, do you?)

B. Simple question with interrogative pronouns (QW): The interrogative pronouns, **shéi** 誰 and **shénme** 什麽, are called question words in this text. The sentence: **Shéi kàn shū?** (Who reads books?) illustrates that the interrogative pronoun can be used as a subject to form a simple question. As for the sentence **Tā shì shéi?** (Who is he?) the interrogative pronoun **shéi** is placed in an object position. In the following sentences: **Shénme guì?** (What is expensive?) **Nǐ kàn shénme ne?** (What are you reading?) We can see that **shénme** is also an interrogative pronoun, used to form questions in the same capacity as the question word **shéi**. In this type of question, the particle **ma** can not be applied.

Pattern 1: <u>QW (A) (A) SV?</u>

      Ex 1: Shénme bú guì?

           什麽不貴?

           (What is not expensive?)

Ex 2: Shéi hěn hǎokàn?

誰很好看？

(Who is very good-looking?)

Pattern 2: S   EV/FV   QW?

Ex 1: Nín shì shéi?

您是誰？

(Who are you?)

Ex 2: Tāmen kàn shénme?

他們看什麼？

(What are they looking at?)

C.　Simple question with positive and negative verb: This is a "yes" or "no" type question. The questions are formed by adding to a positive statement the negative form of the verb such as in **Tā gāo bugāo?** (Is he tall or not?) and you can reply with either "Yes, he is tall," or "No, he is not tall." This is the way to make a positive—negative verb question. Neither interrogative pronoun nor interrogative particle is used.

Pattern 1: S   SV   neg.   SV?

Ex: Nín lèi bu lèi?

您累不累？

(Are you tired or not?)

Pattern 2: S   EV   bu—EV   O?

Ex: Tā shì bu shì lǎoshī?

他是不是老師？

or, S   EV   O,   bu—EV?

Tā shì lǎoshī bushì?

他是老師不是？

(Is he a teacher or not?)

Pattern 3: S   FV   bu—FV   O?

Ex: Nǐ kàn bukàn bào?

你看不看報？

or, S   FV   O,   bu—FV?

Nǐ kàn bào bukàn?

你看報不看？

(Do you read newspapers or not?)

2.5.　Easy Compound Sentence with the Movable Adverb **Kěshì** 可是:　**Kěshì** 可是

21

(but) can be placed either before or after the subject of the second clause in a sentence, as in **Tā gāo kěshi wǒ bù gāo** (He is tall, but I'm not.), **Wǒ hěn lèi, tā kěshi bú lèi** (I'm tired but he/she is not.). The function of **kěshi**, obviously, is to connect two separate but relevant simple sentences together for contrast. Thus, **kěshì** acts as a connector, and can be called a movable adverb (MA) (see note) here. The basic structure is as simple as "clause 1, **kěshi** clause 2." If one clause is positive, the other one must be negative, or the contrast will not exist.

A.   With stative verbs:

Pattern 1: S1 pos./neg. SV, (kěshi) S2 (kěshi) neg./pos. SV.

      Ex 1:   Shū hǎo, kěshi bào bùhǎo.

            書好，可是報不好。

            (Books are good, but newspapers are not.)

      Ex 2:   Wǒ bùgāo, kěshi tā gāo.

            我不高，可是她高。

            (I'm not tall, but she is.)

Pattern 2: S SV1, **kěshi** SV2.

      Ex: Shū hǎokàn, kěshi guì.

          書好看，可是貴。

          (Books are interesting, but expensive.)

B.   With equative verb:

Pattern: N1 pos./neg. EV N2, (kěshi) N3 (kěshi) neg./pos. EV (N2).

    Ex: Wǒ búshì xuésheng, kěshi tā shì (xuésheng).

       我不是學生，可是她是（學生）。

       (I'm not a student, but she is.)

C.   With functive verbs:

Pattern 1: S1 pos./neg. FV O, (kěshi) S2 (kěshi) neg./pos. FV (O).

      Ex: Wǒ kàn bào, kěshi tā bú kàn.

         我看報，可是他不看。

         (I read newspapers, but he doesn't.)

Pattern 2: S pos./neg. FV O1, (kěshi) neg./pos. FV O2.

      Ex: Wǒ kàn nǐmen, kěshi bú kàn tā.

         我看你們，可是不看她。

         (I'm looking at you, but not at her.)

PART V.   GRAMMAR NOTES AND OTHERS

1. <u>Nouns (N)</u>:   Chinese nouns function essentially as sentence subjects, objects or modifiers of other nouns. A noun itself is not specific with respect to number, so that **shū** 書 may refer to "a book" or "books."

2. <u>Personal Pronouns(PN)</u>:   Personal pronouns are one of the three types of pronouns in Chinese. The personal pronouns are like pronouns in English. The ending—men is used as a pluralizer. A personal pronoun does not change in form whether it is in the subjective or objective case.

3. <u>Adverbs (A)</u>:   Adverbs modify verbs, as well as other adverbs which precede verbs. Both negative **bù** 不, and stative verbs may be used as adverbs. The adverb **yě** 也 is a marker of identity and it precedes only a verb or an adverb. **Hěn** 很 is an adverb of degree, which cannot modify a functive verb directly.

4. <u>Movable Adverbs (MA)</u>:   Movable adverbs, like other adverbs, may stand right before the verb or another adverb. They are different from other adverbs in that they may be found before the subject of the sentence. There are three kinds of movable adverbs. **Kěshì** 可是 belongs to the group "pair of conjunction," since it functions to connect two clauses making a compound sentence.

5. <u>Equative Verbs (EV)</u>:   An equative verb, also called a "copula," connects or equates two nouns or nominal phrases, and serves as a center word of the predicate.

6. <u>Stative Verbs (SV)</u>:   Stative verbs describe or characterize nature, status or condition rather than action. In English, this function is performed by the use of "to be" followed by an adjective. In Chinese, the sense of "to be" is embedded in the stative verb. A stative verb can be used as : (1) the center word of a predicate; (2) an adjectival modifier of a noun; (3) an adverbial modifier of a verb. All stative verbs can be modified by **hěn** or other adverbs of degree.

7. <u>Functive Verbs (FV)</u>: Functive verbs express actions or occurances. It is a center word of the predicate. It may have a transitive or intransitive quality.

8. <u>Particles (P)</u>: Particles are those elements which follow a word, a phrase, or a sentence to indicate some particular function or aspect. There are two kinds of particles, one is used as a verb suffix, the other kind is a sentence ending. As a sentence ending, the particle has no specific or concrete meaning. It is the grammatical device employed to impart certain nuances and is called a modal particle. **Ma** 嗎 is a modal particle indicting an interrogative mood. **Ne** 呢 is another modal particle and has four different functions, one of which is to make an abbreviated question.

9. <u>Two Types of Chinese Full Sentences</u>: The very basic word order of a modern Chinese sentence is the pattern "Subject—Predicate." There are two fundamental concepts in the relationship of subject—predicate when considered semantically: (1) topic— comment, the pattern "S SV" is one type among this group; (2) agent action, it seems the pattern of "S FV O" is the only kind right now.

10. <u>Tone Changes on the Negative Adverb Bù—不—</u>: Ordinarily, the negative adverb **bù** — is pronounced with the falling tone. But when **bù**— is immediately followed by another falling tone, **bù** is then changed into a rising tone, e. g. , **búlèi**, **búguì**. In an interrogative sentence with a positivenegative verb, if **bù**— is used as the marker of the negative, it is usually unstressed in rapid speech, so it is seldom audible. Hence, no tone mark is put over the top of **bu**—, e. g. , **hǎo bu hǎo**? In this example only **bu**— is unstressed, but one can also hear that the first verb, which is **hǎo**, is louder than the second **hǎo**.

11. <u>Omission of Tone Marks</u>: Although every Chinese character has a tone, in a sentence the tone of the unstressed syllable may be lost because of the intonation of the sentence. The tone marks can be a guide to both the rhythm and the meaning of a word or a sentence, and therefore, merit the close attention of a beginning student.

12. <u>Chinese Names</u>: In short, the family name stands first and is followed by the given name. The number of Chinese family names is about 400 for Han people; and except for a few surnames which have two syllables, such as **Ōuyáng**, **Sītú**, etc. , all the surnames are one syllable, as in **Gāo**, **Wáng**, **Zhāng**, etc. Many of the given names have two syllables too, but there are also quite a few with only one syllable. Although nowadays

most married women keep and use their maiden names for all occasions, in the old days
a woman's maiden name could not be disclosed to the public. In Taiwan, now it is still
quite common for a married woman to place her husband's surname before her own full
name.

13. Direct Inquires Regarding Surname: The polite way to ask a person for his surname is
to place the word guì 貴 before xìng 姓, as in the phrase: Nín guìxìng? Guì is the respectful way to make a direct inquiry for a person's name, age, and nationality. Lǎo 老
(old) is also a word for a person to show respect for age. Accordingly, one addresses another directly as lǎo xiānsheng (old gentleman), lǎotàitai or lǎo dàniáng (in PRC) for an
old lady. The expression shìde 是的 is also an expression to show a modest attitude when
one is agreeing with what is being said by an older person or one of higher rank.

14. Replying to a Question: In replying to a question, a minor sentence instead of a complete sentence can be used, as long as the content can be understood. However, for a beginner, it is advisable to practice the full sentence first so one can grasp the grammar
more easily and build up a soild foundation.

15. The English Words "A," "The" and "It": They are generally unstressed expressions in
Chinese. In most cases, they are not necessarily given a Chinese equivalent in translation; for example, "I am a teacher" can be translated as Wǒ shì lǎoshī, and a sentence
such as "I'll read it" can be translated as Wǒ kàn; so "it" is not translated when not
stressed.

16. More detailed information related to the sentence structure can be found in the following
chapters of the *Essential Grammar for Modern Chinese*: Chapter II——Words and Parts of
Speech; Chapter V—— Classification of Sentences (2), pp. 63—64; Chapter VI——
The Modification, pp. 73—75; Chapter VIII—The Equative Verb Shì 是, pp. 104—
105; and Chapter XIX——The Modal Particles, p. 272.

PART VI.　　TRANSLATION OF THE TEXT

Books Are Interesting

Student: Good morning! I'm a student. My surname is Gāo. What is your (family) name, please?

Teacher: Good morning! I'm a teacher. My (sur)name is Wáng. What's your (given) name?

Student: My (full) name is Gāo guì.

Teacher: How are you ,Gāo Guì? What are you reading?

Student: Fine. I'm reading a book.

Teacher: Is the book interesting?

Student: Yes it is.

Teacher: Is the book expensive?

Student: Yes, it's expensive, but it's interesting. Newspapers are not expensive, but then newspapers are not fun to read.

Teacher: Who is she? Is she a student?

Student: She is a student. She is very tall and pretty.

Teacher: Are you busy?

Student: Yes, very busy.

Teacher: Do you feel tired?

Student: No, we don't. How about you?

Teacher: I'm busy and tired.

Student: Good-bye, Teacher Wang.

Teacher: Good-bye.

Lesson 3

Auxiliary Verbs, Functive Verbs with Direct Objects, Indirect Objects and Sentence Objects

PART I. TEXT

Dialogue: **Zhōngwén Hǎoxué ma?**--Is Chinese Easy to Learn?

I. *Pinyin* Romanization:

Xuésheng:	Nín hǎo! Wáng lǎoshī.
Lǎoshī:	Nǐ hǎo! Nǐmen máng shénme ne?
Xuésheng:	Wǒmen kàn shū ne.
Lǎoshī:	Nǐmen shì bushì kàn Zhōngwén shū ne?
Xuésheng:	Shìde. Wǒmen dōu xǐhuan kàn Zhōngwén shū.
Lǎoshī:	Nǐmen yǒu Zhōngwén bào ma?
Xuésheng:	Yǒu. Kěshi wǒmen bù xǐhuan kàn Zhōngwén bào.
Lǎoshī:	Zhōngguó fàn ne, hǎochī buhǎochī?
Xuésheng:	Hǎochī. Wǒmen dōu xǐhuan chī.
Lǎoshī:	Zhōngguóhuà hǎoxué, háishi Zhōngguó zì hǎoxué?
Xuésheng:	Zhōngguóhuà hǎoxué. Zhōngguó zì hǎokàn, kěshi bù hǎoxiě.
Lǎoshī:	Wǒ yǒu Zhōngguó shū, yě yǒu Zhōngguó bǐ, nǐmen yào bu yào?
Xuésheng:	Wǒmen yào. Kěshi wǒmen méiyǒu qián.
Lǎoshī:	Wǒ búyào qián, nǐmen gěi bugěi wǒ qián, wǒ dōu

gěi nǐmen shū.

Xuésheng： Xièxie lǎoshī.

Lǎoshī： Búxiè!

II.　Chinese Character Version -- Regular Form：

中　文　好　學　嗎？

學生： 您好！王老師。

老師： 你好！你們忙什麼呢？

學生： 我們看書呢。

老師： 你們是不是看中文書呢？

學生： 是的。我們都喜歡看中文書。

老師： 你們有中文報嗎？

學生： 有。可是我們不喜歡看中文報。

老師： 中國飯呢，好吃不好吃？

學生： 好吃。我們都喜歡吃。

老師： 中國話好學，還是中國字好學？

學生： 中國話好學。中國字好看，可是不好寫。

老師： 我有中國書，也有中國筆，你們要不要？

學生： 我們要。可是我們沒有錢。

老師： 我不要錢，你們給不給我錢，我都給你們書。

學生： 謝謝老師。

老師： 不謝。

III.　Chinese Character Version -- Simplified Form：

28

中文好学吗？

学生：　您好！王老师。
老师：　你好！你们忙什么呢？
学生：　我们看书呢。
老师：　你们是不是看中文书呢？
学生：　是的。我们都喜欢看中文书。
老师：　你们有中文报吗？
学生：　有。可是我们不喜欢看中文报。
老师：　中国饭呢，好吃不好吃？
学生：　好吃。我们都喜欢吃。
老师：　中国话好学，还是中国字好学？
学生：　中国话好学。中国字好看，可是不好写。
老师：　我有中国书，也有中国笔，你们要不要？
学生：　我们要。可是我们没有钱。
老师：　我不要钱，你们给不给我钱，我都给你们书。
学生：　谢谢老师。
老师：　不谢。

PART II.　VOCABULARY——SHĒNGCÍ 生詞

NOUNS (N):

字		zì	character(s), word(s)
飯	饭	fàn	food, meal; rice (cooked)
筆	笔	bǐ	pen; pencil; writing instrument

紙	纸	zhǐ	paper
人		rén	man; people; person
錢	钱	qián	money
一話	一话	-huà	language (spoken), speech
中文		Zhōngwén	Chinese language (both written and spoken)
我的		wǒde	my, mine (**de**, particle indicating possessive case)
你的，您的		nǐde, nínde	your, yours
他的，她的		tāde	his, her, hers
我們的	我们的	wǒmende	our, ours
你們的	你们的	nǐmende	your, yours
他們的	他们的	tāmende	their, theirs
誰的	谁的	shéide	whose
英語	英语	Yīngyǔ	(spoken) English
英文		Yīngwén	English
中國	中国	Zhōngguó	China, Chinese
中國人	中国人	Zhōngguórén	Chinese (people)
美國	美国	Měiguó	America (USA), American
美國人	美国人	Měiguórén	American (people)
外國	外国	wàiguó	foreign country, foreign
外國人	外国人	wàiguórén	foreigner

ADVERBS (A):

没	méi	have not, has not (negative adverb for **yǒu** 有)
		Wǒmen méiyǒu qián.
		我們没有錢。
		(We don't have money.)
都	dōu	all, both, in all cases (see pattern)
		Tāmen dōu hěn gāo.
		他們都很高。

			(All of them are very tall.)
都不—		dōu bù-	none of
			Wǒde shū dōu bú guì.
			我的書都不貴。
			(None of my books are expensive.)
別		bié	don't (imperative voice)

MOVABLE ADVERB (MA):

還是	还是	háishi	or (functions as a conjunction, see pattern)
			Zhōngguóhuà hǎoxué, háishi Yīngyǔ hǎoxué?
			中國話好學,還是英語好學?
			(Which language is easier to study, Chinese or English?)

AUXILIARY VERBS/FUNCTIVE VERBS (AV/FV): The Chinese auxiliary verbs (AV) (see note) correspond roughly to English auxiliary verbs, like "may," "can," etc. It precedes the main verb, e.g. **Tā yào kàn shū.** (He wants to read.) Many auxiliary verbs can also function as ordinary functive verbs, as **yào** 要 and **xǐhuan** 喜歡 in this lesson. **Xǐhuan** can be modified by **hěn** 很.

要		yào (AV/FV)	want, want to; going to; request; demand
			As a FV: Tā yào wǒde bǐ.
			他要我的筆。
			(He wants my pen.)
			As an AV: Tā yào kàn wǒde shū.
			他要看我的書。
			(He wants to read my book.)
喜歡	喜欢	xǐhuan (AV/FV)	like; like to
			As a FV: Nín xǐhuan wǒ ma?

31

您喜歡我嗎？
(Do you like me?)
As an AV: Tā xǐhuan kàn
    Měiguóbào.
她喜歡看美國報。
(She likes to read the
American newspaper.)

FUNCTIVE VERBS (FV):

有		yǒu	have, has

Wǒ yǒu shū, kěshi tā méiyǒu.
我有書，可是她没有。
(I have a book, but she doesn't.)

給	给	gěi	give; give to (gěi can have a person as a receiver who is the indirect object, and a thing which is the direct object (see pattern and note)

Wǒ gěi tā wǒde bǐ.
我給她我的筆。
(I give her my pen.)

寫	写	xiě	write
吃		chī	eat
説	说	shuō	talk, say that (this may have a sentence as its object) (see note)

Tā shuō Zhōngguóhuà.
她説中國話。
(She speaks Chinese.)

學	学	xué	study, learn

Wǒmen dōu xué Yīngyǔ, nǐ ne?
我們都學英語，你呢？

(All of us are studying English, are you?)

STATIVE VERBS (SV):

好＋V		hǎo＋verb	easy to (V), (see note)
好吃		hǎochī	delicious, good to eat
好説	好说	hǎoshuō	easy to speak
好寫	好写	hǎoxiě	easy to write
好學	好学	hǎoxué	easy to learn
有錢	有钱	yǒuqián (SV/VO)	rich; have money
没錢	没钱	méiqián (SV/VO)	poor, not rich; have no money

As a SV: Tā hěn yǒuqián.

他很有錢。

(He is very rich.)

As a VO: Tā yǒu qián, kěshi wǒ méiqián.

他有錢，可是我没錢。

(He is rich, but I am poor.)

VERB-OBJECT COMBINATIONS (VO):

寫字	写字	xiě zì	write (characters)
説話	说话	shuō huà	speak, talk
看書	看书	kàn shū	read
吃飯	吃饭	chī fàn	eat (a meal), have a meal

STRUCTURAL PARTICLE (P):

的	de	(A structural particle whose function here is to indicate a possesive case) (see note)

Wǒmende shū guì.

我們的書貴。

(Our books are expensive.)

EXPRESSIONS (EX):

| 謝謝（您） | 谢谢 | Xièxie (nín) | Thanks, thank you. |
| 不謝 | 不谢 | búxiè | You are welcome. |

NAMES OF A FEW COUNTRIES: (see note)

法國	法国	Fǎguó	France
德國	德国	Déguó	Germany
英國	英国	Yīngguó	England
意大利		Yìdàlì	Italy
日本		Rìběn	Japan
蘇聯	苏联	Sūlián	Soviet Union
西班牙		Xībānyá	Spain

PART III. A LIST OF CHARACTERS REQUIRED TO BE REPRODUCED FROM MEMORY

字 飯 筆 子 人 錢 話 的 中 國 美 外 没 都 有 要
喜 歡 給 寫 吃 學 生 老 師 説 紙

PART IV. SENTENCE PATTERNS

3.1. A Functive Sentence with Yǒu 有: Yǒu 有 is a functive verb, but it does not show any action; it shows ownership. The negative adverb **bù** 不 can not stand before **yǒu**, therefore the negative expression for "do not have" is **méiyǒu** 没有. You may combine it with other words to form stative verbs such as **yǒuqián** (rich), and then it can be modified by **hěn** 很; otherwise the adverb **hěn** cannot stand before **yǒu** immediately.

Pattern: <u>S (méi)yǒu Mod*. O.</u>

Ex 1: Wǒ **méiyǒu** tāde shū.

我没有他的書。

(I do not have his book.)

Ex 2: Tāmen **yǒu** wàiguóqián.

他們有外國錢。

(They have foreign money.)

* "Mod." stands for modification -- see note for more information.

3.2. <u>A Functive Sentence with an Indirect Object and Direct Object</u>: The functive verb **gěi** 給 indicates the agent, which is the subject, and means giving something to someone else. The person who receives the action, or thing, is the indirect object. The indirect object immediately follows the verb **gěi** and precedes the direct object. The indirect object can only be omitted when it is understood from the context.

Pattern: <u>S (bù) gěi I.O. (Mod.) D.O.</u>

Ex 1: Tā **bùgěi** wǒ qián, **gěi** wǒ bǐ.

他不給我錢,給我筆。

(He isn't giving me any money, but is giving me a pen.)

Ex 2: Shéi **gěi** tā shū?

誰給她書?

(Who is going to give her a book?)

Ex 3: Nǐ **gěi** tāmen bào **bugěi**?

你給他們報不給?

(Are you giving them a newspaper?)

Ex 4: Wǒ bù **gěi** tā wǒde shū.

我不給他我的書。

(I'm not going to give him my book.)

3.3. <u>A Simple Sentence with Auxiliary Verb **Yào** 要 or **Xǐhuan** 喜歡</u>: **Yào** 要 and **xǐhuan** 喜歡 both can be used as functive verbs as well as auxiliary verbs. **Xǐhuan**

35

can also be modified by **hěn** 很. When they are used as auxiliary verbs, the pattern is:

Pattern: S (A) AV FV (Mod.) O.

    Ex 1: Shéi **yào** kàn hǎo shū?

        誰要看好書?

        (Who is going to read a good book?)

    Ex 2: Wǒ **yào** shū, kěshi wǒ bú kàn shū.

        我要書,可是我不看書。

        (I want books, but I don't want to read them.)

    Ex 3: Wǒ hěn **xǐhuan** chī Zhōngguófàn.

        我很喜歡吃中國飯。

        (I like to eat Chinese food very much.)

    Ex 4: "Nǐ **xǐhuan** buxǐhuan xué Yīngyǔ?" (Ans.) "**Xǐhuan.**"

        "你喜歡不喜歡學英語?""喜歡。"

        ("Do you like to study English or not?" Ans. "Yes, I like to.")

There are two points worth noting: (1) When a sentence contains two or more verbs, usually you make a negative sentence by using **bù** 不 to negate the first verb; (2) In other words, if a sentence contains an auxiliary and a functive verb, the negative adverb **bù** should be placed before the auxiliary verb to make a negative sentence, e. g., **Wǒmen bù xǐhuan xiě zì.** (We don't like to write characters.)

3.4.   <u>The Totalizing Adverb **Dōu**</u>:   **Dōu** 都 is an adverb which stands before a verb or another adverb, and it is preceded by a plural noun, as in **wǒmen** (we), a collective noun as in **shuǐ** (water), or a series of nouns such as **shū bào** (books and newspapers). The function of **dōu** is to totalize the noun(s) which it follows. When **dōu** is used in a positive sentence, it means "all of" the nouns, as follows: (The use of "dōu" will be further explained in Lesson 12.)

Pattern 1: S **dōu** (neg.) SV.

                  <u>FV (Mod.) O.</u>

    Ex 1: Shū **dōu** hǎokàn.

        書都好看。

        (The books are all interesting.)

    Ex 2: Shū **dōu** bù hǎokàn.

        書都不好看。

        (None of the books is interesting.)

Ex 3: Xuéshengmen **dōu** hěn xǐhuan tā ma?

學生們都很喜歡他嗎?

(Do students all like him very much?)

Ex 4: Xuésheng **dōu** bùxǐhuan tā.

學生都不喜歡他。

(None of the students likes him.)

If the sentence subjects are commonly coupled as a coordination, a connective is not required in Chinese, for example, **nǐ, wǒ** (you and I), and so the above pattern can be rewritten as:

Pattern 2: S1, S2 **dōu** (neg.) SV.

 FV (Mod.) O.

Ex 1: Shū, bào **dōu** hěn guì.

書、報都很貴。

(Books and newspapers are both very expensive.)

Ex 2: Zhōngguóhuà, Yīngyǔ **dōu** bù hǎoxué.

中國話、英語都不好學。

(Neither Chinese nor English is easy to study.)

Ex 3: Lǎoshī, xuésheng **dōu** xǐhuan shuō huà.

老師、學生都喜歡說話。

(Both the teacher and the student like to talk.)

Ex 4: Nǐ, wǒ **dōu** bú kàn wàiguóbào.

你,我都不看外國報。

(Neither of us read foreign newspapers.)

When **bù** occurs right after **dōu**, this phrase can be roughly translated into "none of ..." or "neither...". However, if the position of **dōu bù-** is reversed to **bùdōu** (not all of), this expression should be used only when further information is available right after it. We shall discuss it in Lesson 6 when the pattern of "the whole before the part" is introduced.

3. 5. Functive Verb **Shuō** 說 May Take a Sentence-Object: **Shuō** 說 is one of those verbs which can have a simple object, as in **Tā shuō Zhōngguóhuà** (She speaks Chinese.) as well as carry a sentence as its object. The sentence object of **shuō** may be either a direct or indirect quotation.

Pattern: S **shuō** O.

 (Subject-Predicate).

Ex 1: Tā **shuō**: "Wǒ yǒu bǐ".

他説："我有筆。"

(He said: "I have a pen.")

Ex 2: Tā shuō, tā bùmáng.

他説，他不忙。

(He says that he is not busy.)

3.6.　A Choice Type Question with the Connective Háishi 還是：　The movable adverb **háishì** 還是 (or) serves as a conjunction connecting two relevant sentences together, in order to make an interrogative sentence containing two alternatives. The choice may be between two different subjects or predicates:

A. Choice between two subjects:

Pattern: S1 Predicate, **háishi** S2 Predicate.

Ex 1: Nǐ gāo, **háishi** wǒ gāo?

你高，還是我高？

(Who is taller, you or I?)

Ex 2: Tā bùxiǎng shuō Zhōngguóhuà, **háishi** nǐ bùxiǎng shuō (Zhōngguóhuà)?

他不想説中國話，還是你不想説（中國話）？

(Who doesn't want to speak Chinese, you or he?)

B. Choice between two predicates:

Pattern: S Predicate 1, **háishi** Predicate 2.

Ex 1: Tāde shū hǎo **háishi** bùhǎo?

他的書好還是不好？

(Is his book good, or not?)

Ex 2: Nǐ yào kàn shū, **háishi** yào xiě zì?

你要看書，還是要寫字？

(What do you want to do, read or write?)

PART V.   GRAMMAR NOTES AND OTHERS

1. Auxiliary Verb (AV): We noted in the vocabulary list that **yào** 要 and **xǐhuan** 喜歡 have dual functions--they can be used as auxiliary verbs to express intention, as well as act as functive verbs to show actions. Although, quite a few verbs in Chinese may have this kind of dual function, and may also be modified by **hěn** 很, it is not necessary that every auxiliary verb or functive verb show this nature. The English auxiliary verbs are the counterparts of Chinese optative verbs (or auxiliary verbs); however, the Chinese auxiliary verbs are not consistently translated into auxiliary verbs in English — for instance, the word **yuànyi** 願意 (wish to, Lesson 4) is not. The function of an auxiliary verb is to indicate possibility, ability, willingness, demand or intention. An auxiliary verb is also placed as the first verb in a verbal series in a sentence. None of the auxiliary verbs can be presented in a reduplicated form, although two auxiliary verbs may appear in succession.

2. The Combination of Verb-Object: Transitive verbs in Chinese are commonly found with a generalized object, which is not required in English. **Chī fàn** (to eat a meal) and **kàn shū** (to read a book) are both considered verb-object compounds. A modifier of an object must be inserted between the verb and the object being modified. For example, the expression "eat Chinese food" should be presented as **chī Zhōngguófàn** not as **chīfàn Zhōngguófàn**.

3. Structural Particle **De** 的: In the Chinese language, one can find that there are three kinds of particles. **Ma** 嗎 and **ne** 呢 are modal particles. They are placed at the end of sentences. Structural particles are one of the other two kinds. The structural particle **de** 的 is a neutral tone morpheme and it functions as: (1) a marker of the possessive to indicate possession, as in **lǎoshī de shū** (teacher's book), **wǒde qián** (my money); (2) a marker of subordinate construction in the word order "modification **de** noun," and serves as a connector in the modifier-modified relation. An example from this lesson would be **hěnhǎo de Zhōngguóbǐ**, where the combination of "A-SV" is used as a modifier, the particle **de** is required (see Lesson 8).

4. Some Basic Concepts of Noun Modification:

A.　In the word **Zhōngguórén** 中國人, **Zhōngguó** indicates the origin of the people, and it is clear that the proper noun **Zhōngguó** here is a modifier.

B.　Stative verbs as modifiers of nouns: Usually the monosyllabic stative verbs may be used as the English adjectives to modify nouns, for example, **hǎorén** 好人 (good person). But when a stative verb consists of more than one syllable or is modified by an adverb, the structural particle **de** must be used between the stative verb and the noun, e. g., **hěnhǎo de rén** (very good person).

C.　The combination of **hǎo** + functive verb: When **hǎo** 好 (good) stands before a functive verb and forms the compound **hǎo-FV**, this compound acts as a stative verb with the meaning "good to (FV)" or "easy to (FV)."

5.　The Indirect Objects and Omission of the Tone Marks:　The word order for a sentence containing an indirect object and a direct object, as in **tā gěi wǒmen shū** (he is giving us the book) requires that the indirect object **wǒmen** must follow the verb **gěi**, while it precedes the direct object, **shū**. In general, the tone of the indirect object is unstressed.

6.　More detailed information relating to the structures included in this lesson can be found in *Essential Grammar for Modern Chinese* in Chapter II—Words and Parts of Speech; Chapter V—Classification of Sentences, (1): The Mood; Chapter VI—The Modification, pp. 73-74; Chapter VIII—The Functive Verb **Yǒu** 有, pp. 114-116; and Chapter XI—The Structural Particle **De** 的, pp. 158-160.

PART VI.   TRANSLATION OF THE TEXT

Is Chinese Easy to Learn?

Student: How are you, Teacher Wang!

Teacher: How are you? What are you doing?

Student: We are reading.

Teacher: Are you reading Chinese books?

Student: Yes, we all like reading Chinese books.

Teacher: Do you have the Chinese newspaper?

Student: Yes, we do. But we don't like reading it.

Teacher: How about Chinese food? Do you think it's tasty?

Student: Yes, we all like Chinese food.

Teacher: Which is easier, spoken Chinese or written?

Student: Spoken Chinese is easier. Chinese characters look pretty, but they are difficult to write.

Teacher: I have Chinese books and Chinese pens too. Do you want them?

Student: We want them, but we don't have any money.

Teacher: I won't take your money. I'll let you have the books whether you pay me or not.

Student: Thank you.

Teacher: Don't mention it.

Lesson 4

Specification, Quantification of Nouns; and Transposition of Objects

PART I.   TEXT

Dialogue: **Shuō Zhōngguóhuà**——Speaking Chinese

I.   *Pinyin* Romanization

Gāo Guì:	Nǐ hǎo! Wǒ jiào Gāo Guì, wǒ shì Měiguórén. Nǐ guì xìng?
Qián Dàshēng:	Wǒ xìng Qián, wǒ jiào Qián Dàshēng. Wǒ shì Zhōngguórén.
Gāo Guì:	Qǐngwèn, zhèi zhāng zhuōzi, nèi bǎ yǐzi shì nǐde ma?
Qián Dàshēng:	Bú shì wǒde.
Gāo Guì:	Shì shéide?
Qián Dàshēng:	Wǒ yě bù zhīdào, nǐ wènwen Wáng lǎoshī.
Gāo Guì:	Wǒ bú yuànyi wèn lǎoshī, tā bù dǒng wǒde Zhōngguóhuà.
Qián Dàshēng:	Nǐ bú huì shuō Yīngyǔ ma?
Gāo Guì:	Wǒ bù kěyǐ shuō Yīngyǔ. Wǒ de lǎoshī chángcháng shuō: "Gāo Guì, nǐ xué Zhōngwén, bú yào shuō Yīngyǔ."
Qián Dàshēng:	Wǒ dǒng nǐde yìsi. Nǐ bú yuànyi shuō Yīngyǔ, wǒ xiǎng wèntí bú dà. Wǒ yǒu yì zhāng zhuōzi, yì bǎ yǐzi, kěyǐ gěi nǐ.

Gāo Guì：	Hǎo a！Kěshi wǒ gěi nǐ shénme ne? Nǐ yào qián háishi yào wǒ zhèi gè biǎo?
Qián Dàshēng：	Wǒ xǐhuan kàn wàiguó huàbào, nǐ yǒu méiyǒu?
Gāo Guì：	Wǒ yǒu. Nǐ yào zhèi wǔ běn Měiguóde, háishi nèi liù běn Yīngguóde?
Qián Dàshēng：	Wǒ xiǎng yi xiǎng. Nǐde huàbào dōu hěn yǒu yìsi. Nǐ dōu gěi wǒ, hǎo buhǎo?
Gāo Guì：	Méi wèntí！

II.　Chinese Character Version——Regular Form：

説 中 國 話

高貴：	你好！我叫高貴，我是美國人。你貴姓?
錢大生：	我姓錢，我叫錢大生。我是中國人。
高貴：	請問，這張桌子，那把椅子，是你的嗎?
錢大生：	不是我的。
高貴：	是誰的?
錢大生：	我也不知道，你問問王老師。
高貴：	我不願意問老師，他不懂我的中國話。
錢大生：	你不會説英語嗎?
高貴：	我不可以説英語。我的老師常常説："高貴，你學中文，不要説英語。"
錢大生：	我懂你的意思。你不願意説英語，我想問題不大。我有一張桌子，一把椅子，可以給你。
高貴：	好啊！可是我給你什麼呢?你要錢還是要我這個錶?
錢大生：	我喜歡看外國畫報，你有沒有?
高貴：	我有。你要這五本美國的，還是那六本英國的?

钱大生：　我想一想。你的畫報都很有意思，你都給我，好不好？
高貴：　　没問題。

III.　　**Chinese Character Version——Simplified Form：**

说中国话

高貴：　　你好！我叫高貴，我是美国人。你贵姓？
钱大生：　我姓钱，我叫钱大生。我是中国人。
高貴：　　请问，这张桌子，那把椅子，是你的吗？
钱大生：　不是我的。
高貴：　　是谁的？
钱大生：　我也不知道，你问问王老师。
高貴：　　我不愿意问老师，他不懂我的中国话。
钱大生：　你不会说英语吗？
高貴：　　我不可以说英语。我的老师常常说："高貴，你学中文，不
　　　　　要说英语。"
钱大生：　我懂你的意思。你不愿意说英语，我想问题不大。我有一
　　　　　张桌子，一把椅子，可以给你。
高貴：　　好啊！可是我给你什么呢？你要钱还是要我这个表？
钱大生：　我喜欢看外国画报，你有没有？
高貴：　　我有。你要这五本美国的，还是那六本英国的？
钱大生：　我想一想。你的画报都很有意思，你都给我，好不好？
高貴：　　没问题。

44

PART II. VOCABULARY——SHĒNGCÍ 生詞

SPECIFIERS (SP): (see pattern and note)

這	这	zhě, zhèi	this, these (depends on whether the noun is singular or plural)
			Wǒmen yào kàn zhèběn shū.
			我們要看這本書。
			(We want to read this book.)
那		nèi, nà	that, those
			Nà sān zhāng zhuōzi dōu hěn guì.
			那三張桌子都很貴。
			(Those three tables are all very expensive.)
哪		něi, nǎ	which
			Nǐ yào něige biǎo?
			你要哪個錶？
			(Which watch do you want?)

NUMBERS (NU): A number serves as a counter (see pattern and note).

一		yī	one
二		èr	two
三		sān	three
四		sì	four
五		wǔ	five
六		liù	six
七		qī	seven
八		bā	eight
九		jiǔ	nine
十		shí(NU/M)	ten; a unit of ten
零	零	líng	zero; plus, and
兩	两	liǎng—M (BF)	two; a couple of
			Tā yào liǎngzhī bǐ.

45

			她要兩支筆。 (She wants two pens.)
幾	几	jǐ—M (BF)	how many (for number under ten) Nǐ yǒu jǐzhāng zhǐ? 你有幾張紙？ (How many sheets of paper do you have?)

MEASURES (M): There are two kinds of measure words. One has the same function as its counterpart in English, which is to quantify a noun, as in **liǎng zhāng zhǐ** (two sheets of paper). **Zhāng** is the measure for paper in Chinese. The other kind of measure word is used to indicate the duration of action, which will be discussed in Lesson 13. (See pattern and note.)

個	个	—ge	a general measure word, can be applied to practically anything and everything. Usually **ge** is a neutral tone, but when it is stressed, it has a fourth tone. Tā xǐhuan zhèige biǎo. 他喜歡這個錶。 (He likes this watch.)
本		—běn	volume (for books, pictorials, magazines, etc.) Shéi yào kàn nèiběn huàbào? 誰要看那本畫報？ (Who wants to read that pictorial magazine?)
張	张	—zhāng	sheet, something flat (for paper, painting, table, etc.) Nèizhāng zhuōzi bù xiǎo. 那張桌子不小。 (That table is not small.)
位		—wèi	a polite measure for persons, but cannot be followed by **rén**

directly, as in **yíwèi rén**.

Yíwèi wàiguórén is correct.

Zhèwèi lǎoshī xìng shénme?

這位老師姓什麼？

(What is the surname of this teacher?)

把		—bǎ	(for chairs or things with a handle)

Qǐng gěi wǒ liǎng bǎ dà yǐzi.

請給我兩把大椅子。

(Please give me two big chairs.)

枝	支	—zhī	(for writing instruments)

Nǐ yǒu jǐ zhī bǐ?

你有幾枝筆？

(How many pens do you have?)

NOUNS (N):

桌子		zhuōzi	table (M: **zhāng** 張) (see note)
書桌	书桌	shūzhuō	desk (M: **zhāng** 張)
椅子		yǐzi	chair (M: **bǎ** 把) (see note)
意思		yìsi	meaning; idea (M: **gè** 個)
貴國	贵国	guì guó	your nationality (lit., your honorable country)
問題	问题	wèntí	problem, question, issue (M: **gè** 個)
畫兒	画儿	huàr	painting, picture (M: **zhāng** 張)
畫報	画报	huàbào	pictorial magazine (M: **běn** 本, as a copy)
錶	表	biǎo	watch (M: **gè** 個)

ADVERBS (A):

常常（常）	chángcháng	often, commonly, constantly, always

47

Tā chángcháng gěi wǒ qián.
她常常給我錢。
(She is always giving me money.)

MOVABLE ADVERB (MA):

爲什麼　　为什么　　wèishénme　　why
Wèishénme nǐ bù xǐhuan wǒ.
爲什麼你不喜歡我。
(Why don't you like me?)

因爲　　因为　　yīnwèi...　　because
所以　　　　　suǒyǐ...　　therefore; and so...
(Yīnwèi) nǐ huì kàn Zhōngwén,
suǒyǐ wǒ gěi nǐ Zhōngwén shū.
(因爲)你會看中文,所以我給你中文書
[(Because) you can read Chinese,
therefore, I'm giving you Chinese
books.]

AUXILIARY VERBS (AV):

能　　　　　néng　　can (in the sense of "be
able to")
Wǒ bùnéng chī Zhōngguófàn.
我不能吃中國飯。
(I can't eat Chinese food.)

會　　　会　　huì　　can (in the sense of "know
how to"), be able to
Nǐ huì shuō Fǎguóhuà ma?
你會説法國話嗎?
(Can you speak French?)

可以　　　　kěyǐ　　may, can (in the sense of "be
able to")
Nǐ bù kěyǐ gěi tā wǒde qián.
你不可以給他我的錢。

(You must not give him my money.)

| 願意 | 愿意 | yuànyi | wish to, be willing to, want to |

Wǒ yuànyi gěi nǐ zhège.

我願意給你這個。

(I want to give you this.)

AUXILIARY VERBS / FUNCTIVE VERBS (AV/FV):

想   xiǎng

AV: intend to, be thinking of doing, want to

Nǐ xiǎng chī Zhōngguófàn ma?

你想吃中國飯嗎?

(Do you want to have Chinese food?)

FV: (followed by a noun) think about; miss, long for

Wǒ hěn xiǎng tā.

我很想她。

(I miss her very much.)

FV: (followed by a sentence— object, "xiǎng" itself must be in the positive voice) think)

Tā xiǎng Zhōngguórén dōu hǎokàn.

她想中國人都好看。

(She thinks that all Chinese people are good-looking.)

FUNCTIVE VERBS (FV):

懂   dǒng

understand

Wǒ bùdǒng tāde Zhōngguóhuà.

我不懂他的中國話。

(I don't understand his Chinese.)

49

知道		zhīdao	know, know how, know that
			Wǒ zhīdào tā hěn máng.
			我知道她很忙。
			(I know she is very busy.)
問	问	wèn	ask, inquire (see pattern and note)
			Tā yào wèn nǐ yí ge wèntí.
			他要問你一個問題。
			(She is going to ask you a question.)
			Tā wèn wǒ: "Nèiběn shū shì shéide?"
			他問我:"那本書是誰的?"
			(He asked me: "To whom does the book belong?")
請	请	qǐng	invite, ask to; please (see pattern and note)
			Shéi yào qǐng wǒ chīfàn?
			誰要請我吃飯?
			(Who is going to invite me for dinner?)
			Qǐng nǐ gěi wǒ nèiběn huàbào.
			請你給我那本畫報。
			(Would you please give me that copy of the pictorial magazine?)
畫	画	huà	to paint, to draw
			Wǒ chángcháng huà Zhōngguó huàr.
			我常常畫中國畫兒。
			(I often do Chinese paintings.)

STATIVE VERBS (SV):

對	对	duì	correct, accurate

			Nínde yìsi hěn duì. 您的意思很對。 (What you think is very correct.)
有意思		yǒuyìsi	be interesting Nèige rén hěn yǒuyìsi. 那個人很有意思。 (That person is very funny.)
没意思		méiyìsi	be dull, be boring Zhège bào hěn méiyìsi. 這個報很没意思。 (This newspaper is really boring.)
大		dà	big, large
小		xiǎo	small, little

EXPRESSIONS (EX):

請問	请问	qǐngwèn	May I inquire Qǐngwèn:"Nǎwèi shì Wáng lǎoshī?" 請問:"哪位是王老師?" (May I inquire:"Who is Teacher Wang?")
没問題	一问题	méi wèntí	No problem!
好不好		hǎo buhǎo	How about it? (Is that a good idea?)

PART III. A LIST OF CHARACTERS REQUIRED
TO BE REPRODUCED FROM MEMORY

這 那 哪 兩 幾 個 英 張 桌 椅 意 思 問 常 文 爲
因 所 以 想 能 會 願 懂 知 道 請 畫 大 小

PART IV.   SENTENCE PATTERNS

4. 1.   Quantification of Noun with the Pattern "NU—M—N": A number, a measure word plus a noun may form the construction of "NU—M—N" for indicating the number of articles or persons. The pattern "NU—M—N" presents a nominal expression, and it usually can be used as an object in a sentence. The noun, which is quantified by "NU—M" may be omitted if the context permits:

Pattern: The noun phrase "NU—M—N"
    Ex 1: Wǒ yào kàn **liǎng běn shū.**

        我要看兩本書。

        (I want to read two books.)
    Ex 2: Tā kěyǐ gěi nǐ **sān zhāng zhuōzi.**

        他可以給你三張桌子。

        (He may give you three tables.)

4. 2.   Specification of Nouns with the Pattern "SP—NU—M—N": When a specifier **zhèi** 這, **nà** 那 or **něi.** 哪 is placed before "NU—M—N" to form the pattern of "SP—NU —M—N," this combination indicates a particular group of items, such as **Nà qī ge xuésheng** (those seven students). They can be used as a subject as well as an object in a sentence.

    Pattern: The noun phrase of "SP—NU—M—N"
As Subject: Zhèi wǔ zhī bǐ dōu búguì.

        這五枝筆都不貴。

        (None of these five pens is expensive.)
As Object: Wǒ bù mǎi nà shí běn shū.

        我不買那十本書。

        (I'm not going to buy those ten books.)

4. 3.   The Specifiction of Noun Modified by Pronouns: The pronouns may be used as a modifier and stand before the combination of "SP—NU—M—N" to form a new pat-

tern of "PN—SP—NU—M—N" to point out the possession of the particular group of items. In this pattern, the particle de, the marker of possession, can be omitted.

Pattern: The noun phrase of "PN—NU—M—N"

As Subject: Tā nà sān zhāng huàr dōu bù hǎokàn.

他那三張畫兒都不好看。

(None of those three paintings of his are good-looking.)

As Object: Shéi yào wǒ zhèi liǎng ge xiǎo biǎo.

誰要我這兩個小錶。

(Who wants these two small watches of mine?)

4. 4.　Transposition of Objects:　A sentence object may be transposed to the "topic" position when the relationship between the subject and predicate is of the "Topic—Comment" type.

Pattern: Topic　　　　　　　Comment

　　　　Transposed Object, S (A) (AV) FV.

There are four reasons for using the structure of "Transposition of Objects":

A.　To emphasize the object:

Ex: Nèige biǎo, tā bù gěi nǐ.

那個錶,他不給你。

(He is not willing to give you that watch.)

B.　To contrast the objects:

Ex: Yīngwén wǒ huì, (kěshi) Zhōngwén wǒ búhuì.

英文我會,(可是)中文我不會。

(I can speak English, but not Chinese.)

C.　To contrast the subjects:

Ex: Wàiguóhuà, zhèi liǎng ge rén huì shuō, nèige rén búhuì.

外國話,這兩個人會說,那個人不會。

(These two people can speak a foreign language, that one can't.)

D.　To point out the plurality of object(s):　When a plural object(s) is totalized with dōu 都 in a simple sentence, using the form "transposition of Object" is required.

Ex 1: Shū, bào, wǒ dōu bú kàn.

書、報,我都不看。

(I read neither books nor newspapers.)

Ex 2: Nèige Zhōngguó biǎo, zhèige wàiguó biǎo, tāmen dōu xiǎng yào.

那個中國錶,這個外國錶,他們都想要。

(They want that Chinese watch and this foreign watch.)

However, if transposed objects and the subject of a sentence are both plural, the totalizer dōu 都 may be applied to either subject or object or both. The meaning of the sentence however, may be ambiguous, depending on the context. For instance, the following sentence can be interpreted in three ways:

Shū, bào wǒmen dōu yào.

書、報我們都要。

1. We want books and newspapers.
2. We want a book and a newspaper.
3. We each want books and newspapers.

4.5. The Related Movable Adverbs Wèishénme, Yīnwèi...Suǒyi...: These three adverbs are closely related in use.

A. For question—answer: Wèishénme 爲什麽 introduces a question, and yīnwèi 因爲... suǒyi 所以... introduces the answer.

    Ex Q: Nǐ wèishénme gěi tā shū?

       你爲什麽給他書?

       (Why did you give him a book?)

    A: Yīnwèi tā xǐhuan kàn shū, suǒyi wǒ gěi tā.

       因爲他喜歡看書,所以我給他。

       [Because he likes to read, (therefore,) I gave him a book.]

The order of the two clauses yīnwèi... and suǒyi... may be reversed, and then the word suǒyi can be omitted, as in: Wǒ gěi tā shū, (shì) yīnwèi tā xǐhuan kàn. (I gave him a book, because he liked to read.)

B. For cause and effect: If the sentence is not a response to a previous question, yīnwèi may introduce a cause, followed by a second statement giving the effect.

    Ex: Yīnwèi tā hěn lèi, suǒyi bùnéng huà huàr.

       因爲他很累,所以不能畫畫兒。

       [Because he is very tired, (therefore,) he can not draw.]

In common usage yīnwèi is frequently omitted.

    Ex: Zhōngguózì hěn bù hǎoxiě, suǒyi wǒ bú yuànyi xiě.

       中國字很不好寫,所以我不願意寫。

       (It is very difficult to write Chinese characters, therefore, I do not want to write them.)

4.6. Contrast Qǐngwèn 請問, Qǐng 請, and Wèn 問: Qǐngwèn may be used to raise a question politely, thus it is always followed by an interrogative sentence in the form of a direct quote.

Ex: Qǐngwèn: "Wèishénme nǐ bù xǐhuan tā?"

請問:"爲什麽你不喜歡他?"

(May I inquire: "Why don't you like him?")

Although **qǐng** and **wèn** both can be interpreted as "ask", their usages are quite different. The word **qǐng** may be used to ask someone to do a favor, while the word **wèn** is simply used to ask for information. Hence, **wèn** can take an interrogative sentence as a direct quotation. The following examples show the difference between qǐng and wèn clearly:

Ex: As qǐng: Wǒ qǐng tā gěi wǒ nèibǎ yǐzi.

我請他給我那把椅子。

(I've asked him to give me that chair.)

As wèn: Wǒ wèn tā: "Nèiběn huàbào shì shéide?"

我問他:"那本畫報是誰的?"

(I've asked him: "To whom does that pictorial magazine belong?")

4.7. A "Positive—Negative Verb" Type Interrogative Sentence with **Zhīdao** 知道:

Zhīdao 知道 may have a sentence object. A "Positive—Negative Verb" type question can be applied to both verbs——the main verb, and the verb of the sentence—object.

A. The sentence with a "Positive—Negative **Zhīdao**":

Ex: Nǐ zhīdao buzhīdao wǒ hěn máng?

or: Wǒ hěn máng, nǐ zhīdao buzhīdao?

or: Nǐ zhīdao wǒ hěn máng buzhīdao?

你知道不知道我很忙?

or: 我很忙,你知道不知道?

or: 你知道我很忙不知道?

(You know I'm very busy, don't you?)

In this sentence, the emphasis is placed on "whether you know or not?" That means the speaker seems to know the situation, but wonders if the audience knows it.

B. The "Positive—Negative Verb" structure occurs only in the sentence—object, as in:

Ex: Nǐ zhīdao tā yǒu qián méiyǒu?

你知道他有錢没有?

(Do you know if he has money or not?)

This question shows that the speaker doesn't know the situation, and anticipates that his audience may know.

PART V. GRAMMAR NOTES AND OTHERS

1. <u>Specifiers (SP)</u>:   Specifiers are determinative pronouns. They point out a certain group of nouns. A specifier may be found in the construction "SP — NU — M — N." Sometimes when it is used as a sentence object, it may appear independently if the context permits; for example, **Zhè shì wǒde biǎo.** 這是我的錶. (This is my watch.)

2. <u>Numbers (NU)</u>:   Numbers are nouns that serve as counters and function as numerical determinatives. The numbers introduced in this lesson are numbers of definite quantity. In simple counting or in reading off a list of numbers, or in telephone numbers, they are free forms, as in 2 — 3 — 5 — 0 — 3 — 2 — 0. In other situations they are bound — forms and require measures to complete them, e. g. , **sì zhāng huàr** 四張畫兒 (four paintings). ·In Chinese, **líng** 零 may represent the number "zero," and also may connect two figures together, and function as "plus" or "and" in English; as in the figure $ 30. 25, which can be translated in Chinese as **sānshí kuài líng èr máo wǔ** 三十塊零二毛五. **Shí** is a number, but, in Chinese, it is also used as a measure of the numbers with double digits as in twenty (**èrshí** 二十), thirty (**sānshí** 三十), etc. This means **shí** can be used as a number for "ten," as well as a collective measure for a group of numbers.

3. <u>Measures (M)</u>:   In this lesson, the function of the measures was introduced as the quantification of nouns. In addition, measures can also point out the duration of action. This will be discussed in Lesson 13. There are nouns and numbers which may be used as measures for themselves. The number **shí** (ten) is a typical example. If a noun is used to refer to something without regarding quantity, then the measures are not required; for example, rice, water, money, etc. It is the only case where the measure of nouns can be dropped. In English, there are a number of nouns which are required to have certain types of measurements, such as: one piece of candy, a dozen eggs, etc. , however, none of the English measures are "general" in the sense that they can be applied to any or every thing as the Chinese measure **gè** does. For more information regarding the most commonly used measure for nouns, you may check *Essential Grammar for Modern Chinese*

(pp. 98—100).

4. The usage of —zi 子 and —r 兒: —zi 子 and —r 兒 are suffixes. The suffix —zi, which has the function of signalling a noun, is attached to a number of monosyllabic nouns, and becomes a part of the noun combination, e. g.: **zhuōzi** 桌子 (table), **yǐzi** 椅子 (chair). —r can be very popular in Beijing dialect as a suffix for nouns, as in **huàr** 畫兒 (painting); for measures, as in **fènr** 份兒 (a copy, in Lesson 5), for verbs, as in **wánr** 玩兒 (to play, have fun, in Lesson 6); even for adverbs, as in **hǎohaorde** 好好兒地 (carefully, nicely, in Lesson 16). —r differs from **zi** in two respects: (1) suffix —r is used in speaking or reading aloud, and never included in writing.

5. Bound Forms (BF): They are word elements carrying individual meanings and usually cannot be used independently, e. g. , **liǎng**—M 兩—M (two—).

6. Unstressed **Yíge** 一個 or **Yī**—M: The expression **yíge** 一個 or **yī**—M is stressed only under certain circumstances. Normally, **yí ge** or **yī**—M is an unstressed word with neutral tones. In speaking, the syllable **yī** is often lost, as in **Tā yǒu ge wèntí** 她有個問題 (She has a problem.) and in **Wǒ búyào zhèzhī bǐ** 我不要這枝筆 (I don't want this pen). It seems the unstressed **yí ge** or **yī**—M corresponds to the indefinite article "a" or "an" in English.

7. Use of **Èr** 二 and **Liǎng** 兩: **Èr** 二 is a free form number and is used in counting, while **liǎng** 兩 is a bound form requiring a measure word after it to present a sense of "NU—M" in order to point out the quantification of nouns. Students were advised to use **liǎng**—M only for showing the figure as two of a certain item. However, the evidence found in the Chinese language texts prepared in PRC, indicates that the expression "**èr**—M—N" is a new speaking habit of Chinese people in Mainland China. Hence, we should consider that both forms, **liǎng**—M and **èr**—M, are appropriate.

8. Change of Tone on **Yī** 一, **Qī** 七 and **Bā** 八:

Word When Standing Alone	Before 1st Tone	Before 2nd Tone	Before 3rd Tone	Before 4th Tone
yī	yìzhāng	yìnián *	yìběn	yígè
qī	qīzhāng	qīnián	qīběn	qígè
bā	bāzhāng	bānián	bāběn	bágè

* "Nián" means "year."

57

9. <u>Reduplication of Functive Verbs</u>: A function verb may be used in a reduplicated form to imply short or quick action. Examples are: **xiǎng(yi)xiǎng** 想一想 (think over), **wènwen** 問問 (inquire about something in a casual manner), **xuéxue** 學學 (study for a while). The verb so repeated may lose its tone. Since **yī** 一 is unstressed and not very audible, if it is dropped, the meaning of the word does not change.

10. <u>Usages of the Auxiliary Verbs **Xǐhuan** 喜歡 and **Yuànyi** 願意</u>: As we know, not every Chinese auxiliary verb can be translated into an English auxiliary verb. For instance, **yuànyi** is an AV in Chinese, but its nearest equivalent in English, "wish to," is not. Furthermore, the auxiliary verbs, **xǐhuan** and **yuànyi** may not follow their English counterparts, "like to" and "wish to", either. For instance, the sentence "I would like to give all my money to him." is better translated into Chinese as: **Wǒde qián, wǒ (xiǎng)yào dōu gěi tā** 我的錢,我想要都給他, or **Wǒde qián, wǒ yuànyi dōu gěi tā** 我的錢,我願意都給他 instead of using the word for word translation, **Wǒde qián, wǒ xǐhuan dōu gěi tā** 我的錢,我喜歡都給他. Obviously, **yuànyi** reveals a strong commitment by the speaker, just as **xǐhuan** is not used to show an intention or demand. For the same reason, the Chinese people do not use **nǐ yuànyi**... very often, only when a serious commitment is expected, as in **Nǐ yuànyi gēn wǒ jiéhūn ma?** 你願意跟我結婚嗎? (Are you going to marry me?). Unfortunately, only repeated practice and prolonged exposure will fully develop the students' judgment for their proper use.

11. <u>Using Specifiers **Zhèi**—M 這—M and **Nà**—M 那—M to Express the Stressed "It" or "They" and "Them" (the plurality of it)</u>: In most cases, the English words "it" and its plurality "they" or "them," are not translated into Chinese. Those pronouns are understood, e. g. , "I don't like it," in Chinese, can be said as **Wǒ bù xǐhuan** 我不喜歡. But if the speaker needs to stress those pronouns, he can use either **zhèi**— 這 or **nà**— 那 for emphasis, e. g. , "I don't like it" with emphasis, can be presented in Chinese as **Wǒ bù xǐhuan zhèige** 我不喜歡這個, or **Wǒ bù xǐhuan nèige** 我不喜歡那個.

12. The suggested reading from *Essential Grammar for Modern Chinese* is: Chapter II——Words and Parts of Speech; Chapter III——The Essential Elements of a Sentence; Chapter VII——Determinatives and Measures; and Chapter XVIII——Placing Emphasis Within a Sentence, pp. 257, 259 and 260.

PART VI. TRANSLATION OF THE TEXT

Speaking Chinese

Gao Gui:	How do you do? My name is Gao Gui. I'm from the United States. May I have your family name?
Qian Dasheng:	My family name is Qian, my full name is Qian Dasheng. I'm Chinese.
Gao Gui:	Could you tell me whether this table and that chair are yours?
Qian Dasheng:	No, they are not mine.
Gao Gui:	Then, whose are they?
Qian Dasheng:	I don't know either. You can ask Professor Wang.
Gao Gui:	I don't want to ask the teacher. He doesn't understand my Chinese.
Qian Dasheng:	Don't you know how to speak English?
Gao Gui:	I shouldn't speak English. My teacher often says to me: "Gao Gui, You are learning Chinese. You shouldn't speak English."
Qian Dasheng:	I see, you don't want to speak English. I don't think there's any problem. I have a table and a chair which I can give you.
Gao Gui:	That's fine. But what should I give you, some money or this watch of mine?
Qian Dasheng:	I like to read foreign pictorials. Do you have any?
Gao Gui:	Yes I do. Do you want these five American ones or those six British ones?
Qian Dasheng:	Let me see. All of your pictorials are very interesting. Could you give me all of them?
Gao Gui:	No problem.

Lesson 5

Monetary Expressions, Price, Counting,
Coverb and Verb Compounds

PART I.   TEXT

Dialogue: Mǎi Dōngxi--Shopping

I.   *Pinyin* Romanization:

Zhè shì yí ge shāngdiàn, zhèige shāngdiàn hěn dà, dōngxi yě hěn duō. Gāo Guì xiǎng mǎi shūzhuō, yǐzi, kěshi tā kànkan zhèi zhāng, zhēn guì; kànkan nèi zhāng, bú dà xǐhuan. Tā bù zhīdao mǎi něige, yǒu yí ge diànyuán wèn tā:

Diànyuán:	Nín yào mǎi shénme?
Gāo Guì:	Wǒ yào mǎi yì zhāng shūzhuō, liǎng bǎ yǐzi.
Diànyuán:	Wǒmen yǒu hěnduō zhuōyǐ, dàde, xiǎode dōu yǒu, nín yào něige?
Gāo Guì:	Nǐmende zhuōzi dōu hěn hǎokàn, kěshi guì. Wǒ shì yí ge xuésheng, qián bùduō, wǒ xiǎng mǎi yì zhāng piányide zhuōzi.
Diànyuán:	Xīnde zhuōzi dōu hěn guì, jiùde piányi, nín yào kànkan ma?
Gāo Guì:	Wǒ búdà ài mǎi jiù dōngxi.
Diànyuán:	Nà, nín kàn zhè zhāng ne? Zhǐyao liùshí kuài qián, háiyǒu nà liǎng bǎ yǐzi.
Gāo Guì:	Zhèi liǎng bǎ yǐzi wǒ bù xǐhuan, bù hǎokàn.
Diànyuán:	Zhèi liǎng bǎ kěyǐ ma?
Gāo Guì:	Wǒ yě bù xǐhuan, zhēn ǎi! Duìbuqǐ, hái yǒu biéde ma?

60

Diànyuán :	Yǒu, nèi liǎng bǎ hěn hǎokàn, kěshì, shì jiùde, nǐ yào ma?
Gāo Guì :	Hǎo, nín gào su wǒ duōshao qián?
Diànyuán :	Èrshí bā kuài.
Gāo Guì :	Kěyǐ, kěyǐ. Wǒ yào.
Diànyuán :	Hǎo, wǒ màigěi nín.
Gāo Guì :	Nǐ màigěi wǒ?
Diànyuán :	(xiào) Wǒde yìsi shì màigěi nǐ yǐzi.
Gāo Guì :	(xiào) Duìbuqǐ, wǒ de Zhōngguóhuà búdà hǎo.
Diànyuán :	Zhuōzi shì liùshí kuài, yǐzi shì èrshí bā kuài, yígòng shì bāshí bā kuài.
Gāo Guì :	Wǒ gěi nín Měiyuán háishi Rénmínbì?
Diànyuán :	Dōu kěyǐ.
Gāo Guì :	Hǎo, zhè shì yì bǎi kuài Rénmínbì.
Diànyuán :	Zhǎo nín qián, xièxie nín.

II. Chinese Character Version--Regular Form :

買 東 西

　　這是一個商店,這個商店很大,東西也很多。高貴想買書桌、椅子,可是他看看這張,真貴;看看那張,不大喜歡。他不知道買哪個,有一個店員問他:

店員:　您要買什麼?

高貴:　我要買一張書桌,兩把椅子。

店員:　我們有很多桌椅,大的、小的都有,您要哪個?

高貴:　你們的桌子都很好看,可是貴。我是一個學生,錢不多,我想買一張便宜的桌子。

店員:　新的桌子都很貴,舊的便宜,您要看看嗎?

高貴:　我不大愛買舊東西。

店員:那,您看這張呢?只是六十塊錢,還有那兩把椅子。

高貴：這兩把椅子我不喜歡，不好看。還有別的嗎？

店員：　有，那兩把很好看，可是，是舊的，你要嗎？

高貴：　好，您告訴我多少錢？

店員：　二十八塊。

高貴：　可以，可以。我要。

店員：　好，我賣給您。

高貴：　你賣給我？

店員：　（笑）我的意思是賣給你椅子。

高貴：　（笑）對不起，我的中國話不大好。

店員：　桌子是六十塊，椅子是二十八塊，一共是八十八塊。

高貴：　我給您美元還是人民幣？

店員：　都可以。

高貴：　好，這是一百塊人民幣。

店員：　找您錢，謝謝您。

III.　**Chinese Character Version--Simplified Form：**

买东西

这是一个商店，这个商店很大，东西也很多。高贵想买书桌、椅子，可是他看看这张，真贵；看看那张，不大喜欢。他不知道买哪个，有一个店员问他：

店员：　您要买什么？

高贵：　我要买一张书桌，两把椅子。

店员：　我们有很多桌椅，大的、小的都有，您要哪个？

高贵：　你们的桌子都很好看，可是贵。我是一个学生，钱不多，我
　　　　想买一张便宜的桌子。

店员：　新的桌子都很贵，旧的便宜，您要看看吗？

高贵：　我不大爱买旧东西。

店员： 那，您看这张呢？只要六十块钱，还有那两把椅子。

高贵： 这两把椅子我不喜欢，不好看。

店员： 这两把可以吗？

高贵： 我也不喜欢，真矮！对不起，还有别的吗？

店员： 有，那两把很好看，可是，是旧的，你要吗？

高贵： 好，您告诉我多少钱？

店员： 二十八块。

高贵： 可以，可以。我要。

店员： 好，我卖给您。

高贵： 你卖给我？

店员： （笑）我的意思是卖给你椅子。

高贵： （笑）对不起，我的中国话不大好。

店员： 桌子是六十块，椅子是二十八块，一共是八十八块。

高贵： 我给您美元还是人民币？

店员： 都可以。

高贵： 好，这是一百块人民币。

店员： 找您钱，谢谢您。

PART II.　　VOCABULARY--SHĒNGCÍ 生詞

<u>NUMBERS (NU)</u>:

很多	hěnduō (NU/SV)	many, a lot of (measure word is optional) Tā yǒu hěnduō (běn) shū. 她有很多(本)書。 (She has a lot of books.)
不少	bùshǎo (NU/SV)	not a few (measure word is optional) Shāngdiàn de dōngxi zhēn

			bùshǎo.
			商店的東西真不少。
			(The store carries quite a few goods.)
多少		duōshao	How many? How much? (measure word is optional. It is an interrogative word, and it applies to numbers and amount of any size.)
			Nǐ yǒu duōshao qián?
			你有多少錢?
			(How much money do you have?)
幾—M	几—M	jǐ-M	a few (two to ten), some (jǐ sometimes loses its tone to make a statement)
			Nín kěyǐ gěi wǒ jǐ kuài qián ma?
			您可以給我幾塊錢嗎?
			(Would you give me a few dollars?)
好幾—M	好几—M	hǎojǐ-M	quite a few
			Tāde hǎojǐ běn huàbào dōu hěn yǒuyìsi.
			他的好幾本畫報都很有意思。
			(Quite a few pictorial magazines of his are very interesting.)

NUMBERS/MEASURES (NU/M): The words below can be classified in the same category as "shí 十" (ten) mentioned in Lesson 4 (see note).

百		bǎi	hundred; a unit of hundred
千		qiān	thousand; a unit of thousand
萬	万	wàn	ten thousand; a unit of ten thousand

MEASURES (M):

塊	块	kuài	a piece; (for dollars)
毛		máo	(for dimes)

分		fēn	(for cents)
份兒	份儿	fènr	(for newspaper, magazines)

NOUNS (N):

商店		shāngdiàn	store, shop (M：gè 個, jiā 家)
東西	东西	dōngxi	thing (M：gè 個, jiàn 件)
店員	店员	diànyuán	store clerk, sales personnel
			(M：gè 個, wèi 位)
價錢	价钱	jiàqian	price
別的		biéde	another (person, thing)

Wǒ bù mǎi biéde dōngxi.

我不買別的東西。

(I won't buy any other things.)

別人	biéren	other people (see note)

Biéren dōu shuō yǒuyìsi, kěshi
tā shuō méiyìsi.

別人都説有意思，可是她説没意思。

(Everyone else says it is
interesting, but she says
it's not.)

ADVERBS (A):

不大	búdà	not very

Dōngxi de jiàqian búdà piányi.

東西的價錢不大便宜。

(The prices of things are not low.)

一共	yígòng	all together

Wǒ yígòng yǒu èrshí jǐge
wàiguó xuésheng.

我一共有二十幾個外國學生。

(All together, I have twenty
some foreign students.)

只	zhǐ	only, just, merely

Wǒ zhǐ yǒu yì běn shū.

(I only have one book.)

真　　　　　zhēn　　　　really, quite

Zhèiběn shū zhēn guì.

這本書真貴。

(This book is really expensive.)

AUXILIARY VERBS (AV):

得　　　　　děi　　　　　have to, must (cannot be negated by bù-)

Wǒ děi wènwen nǐ, nǐ nèige biǎo de jiàqian.

我得問問你，你那個錶的價錢。

(I must ask you about the price of that watch of yours.)

不必　　　　búbì　　　　need not, not have to (used as negative of "děi")

Nǐ búbì gàosu wǒ nǐ ài shéi.

你不必告訴我你愛誰。

(You don't have to tell me whom you love.)

AUXILIARY VERB/FUNCTIVE VERB/NOUN (AV/FV/N):

愛　　愛　　ài　　　　　like to, love to; like, love;
　　　　　　(AV/FV/N)　love

Wǒ bú ài nèige rén.

我不愛那個人。

(I don't love that person.)

FUNCTIVE VERBS (FV):

告訴　　告诉　　gàosu　　tell, inform

Tā gàosu wǒ nèiwèi lǎoshī xìng Zhāng.

她告訴我那位老師姓張。

(She told me that the surname
of that teacher is Zhang.)

算	算	suàn	figure, count, calculate
算（一）算		suàn(yi)suàn	figure out, count

Qǐng nǐ suànsuàn, wǒmen
yígòng yǒu duōshao rén.
請你算算，我們一共有多少人。
(Please figure out how many
people we are all together.)

買	买	mǎi	buy

Nǐ búbì mǎi hěnduō dōngxi.
你不必買很多東西。
(You don't have to buy a lot
of things.)

給…買…	给…买…	gěi...mǎi...	buy something for somebody

Nín kěyǐ gěi wǒ mǎi yì běn
huàbào ma?
您可以給我買一本畫報嗎？
(Could you buy a copy of the
pictorial magazine for me?)

賣	卖	mài	sell

Něige shāngdiàn mài piányi
de biǎo?
哪個商店賣便宜的錶？
(Which store sells inexpensive
watches?)

賣給	卖给	màigěi	sell to

Tā màigěi wǒ hěnduō dōngxi.
他賣給我很多東西。
(He sold many things to me.)

找		zhǎo	give change; to find, to look for

Wǒ zhǎo nín yí kuài.
我找您一塊。
(I'll give you ＄1 change.)

笑		xiào	smile, laugh

Nǐ wèishénme xiào?

你爲什麽笑？

(Why are you laughing?)

STATIVE VERBS (SV):

多   duō(BF)   many, much, more (see note)

Hěnduō rén dōu xǐhuan tā.

很多人都喜歡她。

(Many people like her.)

少   shǎo(BF)   few, little, scarce, less (see note)

Rén duō, fàn shǎo.

人多，飯少。

(There are many people, but little food.)

矮   ǎi   be short, be low

Zhèi zhāng zhuōzi zhēn ǎi.

這張桌子真矮。

(This table is very low.)

便宜   piányi   inexpensive; cheap

Piányide bù hǎo, hǎode bù piányi.

便宜的不好，好的不便宜。

(The cheap things are not good enough, the good ones aren't cheap--You get what you pay for.)

新   xīn   be new

Wǒ yào yì bǎ xīn yǐzi.

我要一把新椅子。

(I need a new chair.)

舊 旧   jiù   be old (worn), used

Tā búyào jiùde dōngxi, yào xīnde.

她不要舊的東西，要新的。

(She doesn't want the old stuff, she wants the new ones.)

够		gòu	be enough, be sufficient (see note)
			Nínde qián gòu bu gòu?
			您的錢够不够?
			(Do you have enough money?)

INTERJECTIONS (I): Interjections in Chinese, like those in other languages, present only moods rather than express definite thought (see note).

| 哦 | | ò; ó | Oh! Is that really so? |
| 啊 | | à | Oh! |

EXPRESSIONS (EX):

對不起	对不起	Duìbuqǐ	I'm sorry!
對不對	对不对	Duì buduì	Is it correct?
那		nà	in that case

MONETARY TERMS:

美元(金)		Měiyuán(jīn)	U.S. dollars (lit., American gold)
人民幣	人民币	Rénmínbì	Chinese currency in PRC (lit., people's treasury notes)
新臺幣	新台币	Xīn Táibì	Chinese currency in Taiwan (lit., new treasury notes in Taiwan)

PART III.　A LIST OF CHARACTERS REQUIRED
TO BE REPRODUCED FROM MEMORY

多 少 百 千 萬 塊 毛 分 商 店 東 西 別 共 只 得

必 告 訴 算 賣 找 便 宜 新 舊 够 謝 啊 錶 買 愛
真

PART IV.   SENTENCE PATTERNS

5. 1.   Counting Numbers：

A.   With definite quantity：   A difficulty in converting figures from English into Chinese lies in the fact that, while the Arabic system uses four-digit units, in Chinese, every five digits make up a unit, e. g. , 10,000 is ten thousand in English, but is **yí wàn** 一萬 in Chinese. Thus, larger numbers in Chinese are read quite differently from English. **Wàn** is a number and it is also a measure for a unit of ten-thousand. **Bǎi** 百 (hundred) and **qiān** 千 (thousand) are the same as **wàn** 萬. Therefore, these Chinese numbers：**shí** 十, **bǎi** 百, **qiān** 千 and **wàn** 萬 are also numerical measures. They may be presented in definite quantities.

1. Numbers between 11 and 99 with numerical measure **shí** 十：

Pattern：   "shí-NU"   e.g.：**shí·èr** 12   **shíqī** 17

"NU-shí   **èrshí** 20   **qīshí** 70   **jiǔshí** 90

"NU-shí-NU"   **bāshí liù** 86   **jiǔshí jiǔ** 99

2. Numbers between 100 and 9999 using the numerical measure **bǎi** 百 and **qiān** 千.

a. The figure is composed of a series of "number-measure" elements ending in a digit, and carries no "zero."

Pattern：NU1-qiān-NU2-bǎi-NU3-shí-NU4 (digit)

Ex 1：**sānqiān-qībǎi-wǔshí-sì** 3754

Ex 2：**bābǎi-sìshí-èr** 842

b. When **líng** (zero) replaces one or more "number-measure" elements in a series, no measure is used after **líng**, or in the middle of the series. If **líng** appears more than one time, it is read only once. **Líng** is omitted if its position is in the final digit. You can practice this using the following figures：

309   **sānbǎi líng jiǔ**

4027	sìqiān líng èrshí qī
5001	wǔqiān líng yī
9700	jiǔqiān qī(bǎi)
690	liùbǎi jiǔ(shí)

From the figures 9700 and 690, we can see that not only can **líng** be dropped, but also the smallest numerical measure can be omitted from their respective figures if the speaker wishes. This is a very popular abbreviation used in counting numbers.

3. Higher numbers: Start from ten thousand. Since the Chinese tradition is to use five digits as a unit of numbers and since the fifth digit from the right to left is **wàn** 萬, so, **wàn** can also be considered as "one unit of **wàn**." If there is a figure of six digits, it should be called shíwàn 十萬. The comparison between English and Chinese is as follows:

10,000	yíwàn
100,000	shíwàn
1,000,000	yìbǎiwàn
10,000,000	yìqiānwàn
100,000,000	yíwànwàn (or yíyì, since **wànwàn**＝**yì** 億)
1,000,000,000	**shíwànwàn** (or **shíyì**)

Ex: **Zhōngguó yǒu shíyīwànwàn (or shíyīyì) rén.**

中國有十一萬萬（十一億）人。

(China has a population of 1.1 billion people.)

B. The approximate numbers: There are many ways to present approximate numbers, but the most common one is using two neighboring numbers, such as: **liù-qī ge dōngxi** 六七個東西 (six or seven things), **sì-wǔshí běn shū** 四五十本書 (forty or fifty volumes of books), **liǎng-sānbǎi zhāng zhǐ** 兩三百張紙 (two or three hundred sheets of paper).

C. The indefinite quantity with the numbers **duōshao** 多少, and **jǐ-M** 幾-M: **Duōshao** 多少 and **jǐ-M** 幾-M are interrogative numbers for making a question according to the pattern of "QW-N," but there are some distinctions between them.

1. **Jǐ** 幾 is used when the figure expected from a reply is from zero to nine, while **duōshao** can range from the number "zero" to infinity.

2. **Jǐ** 幾 requires a measure, but for **duōshao** 多少, the measure is optional. For instance, the interrogative sentence, "How many dollars do you have?", can be translated as: (1) **Nǐ yǒu jǐ kuài qián?** 你有幾塊錢?, if the expected answer is less than ten dollars; or (2) **Nǐ yǒu duōshao (kuài) qián?** 你有多少（塊）錢, for which the figure of the expected answer can be any number.

3. **Jǐ-M** 幾-M can only be applied to an article which is countable, but **duōshao**

71

has no such restriction.

4.   Jǐ-M 幾-M may stand before or after the numerical measure, e. g. , **Nǐmen yǒu jǐ bǎi běn shū?** 你們有幾百本書？(How many hundreds of books do you have?) but **duōshao** cannot do so.

Since the statement form of jǐ-M 幾-M is in fact the interrogative, jǐ-M being unstressed loses its tone. Jǐ-M cannot be considered as a question word, but is an indefinite number with the range from zero to nine. Following are some examples:

Ex 1: Making questions

jǐge?	How many?
èrshí jǐ?	How many more than twenty?
jǐshí?	How many tens?

Ex 2: Making statements

jǐge	several
èrshíjǐ	twenty some
jǐshí	several tens

5. 2.   <u>Monetary Expressions</u>:   Monetary measures are **kuài** 塊 for dollars, **máo** 毛 for dimes and **fēn** 分 for cents. Because all of these measures have other more general uses, it is important to keep the noun **qián** 錢 (money) in the monetary expressions, unless the idea is clear from the context, or when all measures used refer to certain monetary expressions.

Pattern: NU1-kuài -NU2-máo -NU3-fēn qián

Ex: sān kuài qī máo wǔ fēn qián ($ 3. 75)

sìbǎi èrshí yī kuài (líng) sān máo liù fēn qián ($ 421. 36)

Here **líng**, functions as a connective with the meaning of "and" or "plus," connects two figures together: the larger amount of dollars and the small change.

If the situation is clearly indicated by the context, an abridged form can be applied. For instance:

Question: Nín yǒu duōshao Měiyuán?

您有多少美元？

(How much American money do you have?)

Answer: Wǒ yǒu sān qiān yībǎi wǔshí èr kuài líng

sì máo wǔ fēn qián.

我有三千一百五十二塊零四毛五分錢。

(I have $ 3,152. 45.)

Since the answer is quite wordy, it can be shortened to:

Wǒ yǒu sān qiān yībǎi wǔshí èr kuài sì máo wǔ.

Both the smallest measure **fēn** and the noun **qián** are dropped. You may also just drop the noun **qián**, but keep the measure **fēn** in the sentence. Once the measure **fēn** or any other smallest measure in a particular monetary expression is dropped, the noun **qián** must be omitted as well.

5.3.   Amount Per Unit   There are two ways to express the price of goods or show the purchasing power of money. Each way uses a particular kind of verb(s), although in most cases the main verb is dropped.

A.   The price of goods:

Pattern 1: Goods   Cost   Money

        NU-M-N (wài, shì, yào, děi) NU-M-N

Although there are four verbs: **mài** 賣, **shì** 是, **yào** 要, and **děi** 得, which may be used for "ask for" or "cost," but the sentence can present a clear idea without a main verb.

Ex 1: Yì zhāng zhuōzi (mài) yìbǎi wǔshíjiǔ kuài jiǔ.

一張桌子(賣)一百五十九塊九。

(A table costs $159.90.)

Ex 2: Sān bǎ yǐzi yígòng (yào) duōshao qián?

三把椅子一共(要)多少錢?

(How much for three chairs altogether?)

The expression of "NU-M" of the goods can be moved to the end of the sentence without changing the sense of the sentence. This pattern can be rewritten as:

Pattern 2: Goods   Cost   Money / Unit

        N (mài, yào, shì, děi) money/NU-M

Ex: Zhuōzi (děi) yìbǎi wǔshíjiǔ kuài jiǔ yì zhāng.

桌子(得)一百五十九塊九一張。

(The tables cost $159.90 each.)

B.   The purchasing power of money: How many goods can be bought by a certain amount of money? It can be shown by the following pattern:

Pattern 3: Money   Buys   Units of Goods

        NU-M-N (mǎi)   NU-M-N.

So far, **mǎi** 買 is the only verb we can use in the pattern, if the main verb is kept in the sentence:

Ex: Yí kuài qián (mǎi) sān zhī bǐ.

一塊錢(買)三枝筆。

(A dollar buys three pens.)

C. Apportionment of goods among people:

Pattern 1: Number of People   Action   Units of Things

NU-M-ren (yǒu, yào, mǎi, kàn) NU-M-N.

Ex: Yí ge rén yǒu yí ge biǎo.

一個人有一個錶。

(Each person has a watch.)

Also the object can be transposed as follows:

Pattern 2: O, NU-M-rén FV NU-M.

Ex: Biǎo, yíge rén yǒu yí ge.

錶,一個人有一個。

(As for watches, each person has one.)

5.4. <u>More Information about Functive Verbs with Sentence Object</u>: A sentence that contains a Sentence-Object is an embedded sentence. The main verb of this kind of sentence must be a functive verb able to carry a clause as its object. So far, the verbs introduced in this lesson, with this kind of capability, are: **shuō** 説 (talk, say), **xiǎng** 想 (think), **zhīdao** 知道 (know that), **wèn** 問 (inquire, ask), **gàosu** 告訴 (tell, inform), and **qǐng** 請 (ask). These verbs can be divided into three groups according to their characteristics:

A. Functive verbs that can take indirect objects and sentence—objects: **wèn** 問 and **gàosu** 告訴 belong to this group.

Pattern: S   wèn/gàosu   O.

(S   V   O).

Ex 1: Tā wèn wǒmen: Nèige shāngdiàn de dōngxi piányi bu piányi?

他問我們:"那個商店的東西便宜不便宜。"

(He asked us: "Are the things in that store cheap or not?")

Ex 2: Wǒ gàosu nǐ: "Wǒ bú yuànyi màigei nǐ wǒde shū."

我告訴你:"我不願意賣給你我的書。"

(I tell you that I don't want to sell my book to you.)

B. Functive verbs that can take sentence-objects, but not indirect object: **Shuō** 説, **xiǎng** 想 and **zhīdao** 知道 are in this category.

Ex 1: Wǒ shuō: "Nèige biǎo zhēn bù hǎo kàn, búyào mǎi."

我説:"那個錶真不好看,不要買。"

(I say："That watch is really ugly. Don't buy it.")

Ex 2：Tā **xiǎng** xuésheng dōu méiyǒu hěnduō qián.

他想學生都没有很多錢。

(He doesn't think that students have a lot of money.)

Ex 3：Wǒmen **zhīdao** tā shì yí wèi lǎoshī.

我們知道他是一位老師。

(We know that he is a teacher.)

C. The functive verbs that form causative sentence：Causative sentences are used to make a request, grant permission or state refusal. In the sentence **Wǒ qǐng tā gěi wǒ yì běn shū** 我請他給我一本書 (I've asked him to give me a book.), the sentence subject **wǒ** causes **tā**, which is the subject of the objective clause, to perform the act of " giving me a book" (**gěi wǒ yì běn shū**). In terms of sentence structure, **tā** is the object of **wǒ qǐng** and also the subject of the clause **tā gěi wǒ yì běn shū**.

Pattern：Subject　　　Predicate

　　　　　S　　　FV　　　O.

　　　　　(S　　V　　O).

Ex：　Wǒmen **qǐng** tā xiě jǐ ge Zhōngguózì.

我們請他寫幾個中國字。

(We've asked him to write some Chinese characters.)

5.5.　The Usage of "Gěi 給"：

A.　As functive verb, **gěi** 給 is used as a main verb in a sentence, e. g., "**Wǒ bùgěi tā zhège.** 我不給她這個。"(I won't give her this.)

B.　As a verb suffix of the verb compound **màigěi** 賣給 (sell to)：**Mài**, the first verb, indicates the type of action, while **gěi**, the second verb, shows to whom the action is rendered.

Pattern：S　màigěi　I O　D O.

Ex：　Tā **màigěi** wǒ tāde huàr.

他賣給我他的畫兒。

(He has sold his paintings to me.)

C.　As a coverb in the structure of "CV-N-FV"：　Consider **Wǒ gěi nǐ mǎi yì běn shū.** 我給你買一本書。(I'll buy you a book.) **Mǎi** is a functive verb and the main verb in this sentence. The English counterpart of **gěi** is not "give", but "for", which is a preposition in English. In English, a prepositional phrase is usually placed toward the end of a sentence and not before the main verb. However, most Chinese coverbs

75

may serve the same function as the prepositions in English, although the Chinese coverbs, along with their nouns, are placed before the main verbs.

Pattern: <u>S (A) (AV) CV-N FV (Mod.) O.</u>

or <u>S (A) (AV) gěi-Person mǎi (Mod.) O.</u>

    Ex: Tāmen yào **gěi** nǐ **mǎi** huàbào.

    他們要給你買畫報。

    (They are going to buy some pictorial magazines for you.)

PART V.　　GRAMMAR NOTES AND OTHERS

1.　<u>Interjections (I)</u>:　The interjectional expressions have expressive value to show the speakers' emotion. The interjections are free forms with no tone, but have definite intonation. Except for the word **a** 啊, most interjections are not modal particles. In other words, they cannot appear at the end of a sentence.

2.　<u>Verb Compounds</u>:　The expression **màigěi** 賣給 contains two syllables, but it differs from other disyllabic verbs such as **zhīdao** 知道 (know), **gàosu** 告訴 (tell). **Màigěi** is a combination of two separate verbs, and each of them retains its own meaning and function. **Mài** (sell) shows what kind of action the agent is taking, while **gěi** (here meaning "to") identifies the person who is receiving that action. Hence, a verb compound consists of two or more verbs, the first indicating the main action, and the rest acting as a verb suffix to provide further information relating to the action.

3.　<u>Post Verbs (PV)</u>:　**Gěi** 給 is a verb suffix of the verb compound **màigěi**. A verb suffix, which originally is a verb, follows a functive verb and indicates a certain relationship. This kind of verb suffix is called a "Post Verb."

4.　<u>Coverb (CV)</u>:　The expression **gěi... mǎi...** 給 … 買 … (buy something for somebody) shows that a coverbial expression consists of a coverb and its object. This expression functions as a prepositional phrase functions in English. Although **gěi** 給, along with many other functive verbs, can be used as coverbs, not every coverb may function as a functive verb. A coverbial phrase (or prepositional phrase) may stand before a main verb to modify it. The coverbs cannot be modified by **hěn** 很 (very), but may use **bù**-

or other negative markers to make negative sentences.

5. Usage of **Biéde** 別的 and **Biéren** 別人 as "Other": **Biéde rén** can be shortened to **biéren**. The words **biéde** 別的 and **biéren** 別人 may be used only under the condition of the word "other" being used in the general sense of "different," e. g., **méiyǒu biéren** 沒有別人 (there's no one else), **Wǒ bù xǐhuan biéde** 我不喜歡別的 (I don't like anything else.) However, in the specific sense of "the other," it is expressed by the specifier **nèi** with the appropriate measure. The English sentence "It isn't her, it's the other person." would be translated into Chinese as, **Búshì tā, shì nèige rén.** 不是她，是那個人。

6. Totals: The adverb **yígòng** 一共 (total) appears before expressions of amount or price, which may be optionally preceded by the verb **shì** 是, **yǒu** 有, or **yào** 要.

Ex 1：Wǒmen yígòng (shì/yǒu) wǔ ge rén.

我們一共（是/有）五個人。

(Altogether, we are a group of five.)

Ex 2：Nèi sān ge biǎo yígòng (shì/yào) liǎngbǎi kuài qián.

那三個錶一共（是/要）兩百塊錢。

(Altogether, those three watches cost ＄200.00.)

7. The Expressions of "SV—de": A noun can be modified by a stative verb to form the construction of SV — de — N, such as **piányi de yǐzi** 便宜的椅子 (an inexpensive chair), **hǎokàn de xuésheng** 好看的學生 (a good-looking student). When the context permits, the modified noun may be omitted, in that case, the particle **de** 的 is always present. "SV—de" is a noun phrase and may be substituted for the original "SV—de—N" expression.

8. Stative Verbs of Restricted Function: In general, a stative verb may have three potential functions：(1) to be a predicate, (2) to modify a noun, and (3) to modify a verb. However, some stative verbs, such as **duō** 多, **shǎo** 少 and **gòu** 夠, cannot perform all three functions. **Duō** and **shǎo** are restricted in that they can only modify nouns with another adverbial modifier before them, e. g., the Chinese equivalent of "many people" is **hěnduō rén**, not **duōrén**. **Gòu** and **hěngòu** cannot be used as noun modifiers. Therefore, **Wǒde qián búgòu** 我的錢不夠 (My money is not sufficient.) is the proper way of saying "I don't have enough money."

9. Chapter II——Words and Parts of Speech; Chapter III——The Essential Elements of a

Sentence; and Chapter VII — — Determinatives and Measures of *Essential Grammar for Modern Chinese*, are the related chapters to this lesson and are suggested reading.

PART VI.　TRANSLATION OF THE TEXT

Shopping

This is a shop, and it's a big one. A lot of things are sold here. Gao Gui wants to buy a desks and chairs. Looking at one set, he feels it's too expensive. He sees another, but it doesn't appeal to him. He doesn't know which to buy. At this moment, a salesclerk asks him:

Salesperson: Can I help you?

Gao Gui: Yes, I want to buy a desk and two chairs.

Salesperson: We have many desks and chairs, both small ones and big ones. Which one do you want?

Gao Gui: All your desks are very nice but expensive. I'm a student, and don't have much money. I want to buy a desk which is inexpensive.

Salesperson: New tables are all expensive, while old ones are cheap. Do you want to have a look?

Gao Gui: I don't really like old things.

Salesperson: Then how about this? It costs only sixty yuan. And how about those two chairs?

Gao Gui: I don't like those two chairs. They're ugly.

Salesperson: Then how about these two?

Gao Gui: No, they are too short. Excuse me, do you have any others?

Salesperson: Yes. Those two are beautiful, but they are used. Do you want them?

Gao Gui: Good! Can you tell me how much they cost?

Salesperson: Twenty-eight yuan.

Gao Gui: Ok. I'll take them.

Salesperson: Okay. I'll sell to you.

Gao Gui: You'll sell yourself to me?

Salesperson: (laughing) I mean that I'll sell the two chairs to you.

Gao Gui:	(laughing) I'm so sorry. My Chinese is not good enough.
Salesperson:	The desk is sixty *kuai*. The chairs twenty-eight kuai. That makes eighty-eight *kuai* all together.
Gao Gui:	Should I give you American dollars or Renminbi?
Salesperson:	Either is fine.
Gao Gui:	Good. Here's one hundred *kuai* Renminbi.
Salesperson:	Here's your change. Thank you.

Lesson 6

Yǒu for Existence, Indefinite Determinatives, and Verb Suffix Le

PART I.   TEXT

Dialogue: **Kàn Péngyou** --To Visit a Friend

I.   *Pinyin* Romanization:

Qián Dàshēng:	À! Xiǎo Gāo, qǐngjìn, qǐngjìn!
Qián tàitai:	Huānyíng, huānyíng!
Qián Dàshēng:	Gāo Guì, wǒ gěi nǐ jièshao jièshao, zhèi shì
	wǒ māma, zhèishì wǒ bàba. Zhèi wèi gāode shì
	wǒ jiějie, jiào Dàměi; ǎide jiào Xiǎozhēn, shì
	wǒ mèimei, nà shì wǒ dìdi jiào Èrzhōng, wǒ jiā yǒu
	liù ge rén.
Gāo Guì:	Qián tàitai, Qián xiānsheng hǎo! Xiǎozhēn, Dàměi,
	Èrzhōng, nǐmen hǎo!
Qián tàitai:	Dàshēng gàosu wǒmen, tā yǒu yí gè hǎo péngyǒu
	jiào Gāo Guì. Rén hěn hǎo, yě hěn hǎokàn.
	Wǒmen dàjiā dōu xiǎng rènshirènshi nǐ ne.
	Qǐng zuò, qǐngzuò, qǐng hē chá, chī yìdiǎnr
	táng, biékèqì.
Gāo Guì:	Qián tàitai, nín tài kèqì le.
Dàměi:	Xiǎo Gāo, nǐ bú rènshi wǒ le? Wǒ mài gěi nǐ yì zhāng
	zhuōzi, liǎng bǎ yǐzi...
Gāo Guì:	Ò, nǐ shì shāngdiàn de nèi wèi nǚ tóngzhì ya!
	Zhēn duìbuqǐ, wǒ bù zhīdào nín shì Xiǎo Qián de jiějie.

Qián Dàshēng:	Nà, méi shénme.
Gāo Guì:	Xiǎozhēn xiǎojie yě gōngzuò ma?
Xiǎozhēn:	Wǒ bù gōngzuò, wǒ shì xuésheng.
Gāo Guì:	À, wǒ zhīdao le.
Qián tàitai:	Nǐ jiāde rén dōu hǎo ma?
Gāo Guì:	Dōu hǎo.
Qián tàitai:	Nǐ yǒu xiōngdì jiěmèi ma?
Gāo Guì:	Méiyǒu, wǒ fùmǔ zhǐyǒu wǒ yí ge háizi.
	Suǒyǐ, wǒ de fùwǔ hěn xiǎng wǒ.
Qián tàitai:	Nǐ yǒu àirén ma?
Qián Dàshēng:	Xiǎo Gāo, zhèshì wǒmende shuōfa, "ài rén"
	de yìsi, búshì nǚpéngyou, yě búshì nánpéngyou,
	shì wèn nǐ yǒu méiyǒu tàitai?
Gāo Guì:	Wǒ méiyǒu.
Èrzhōng:	Gēge! Nǐ rènshì hǎoxiē nǚ háizi, wǒ kàn nǐ
	gěi Xiǎo Gāo jièshao yí gè nǚ péngyou ba.
Gāo Guì:	(xiào) Wǒ zhīdao, Zhōngguóde shuōfa jiào
	"jièshào duìxiàng".
Qián Dàshēng:	Duì, wǒmen yào gěi nǐ jièshao yígè duìxiàng!
Gāo Guì:	(xiào) Nà, nà tài hǎo le!

II. Chinese Character Version--Regular Form:

看朋友

錢大生:	啊！小高，請進，請進！
錢太太:	歡迎，歡迎！
錢大生:	高貴，我給你介紹介紹，這是我媽媽，這是我爸爸。這位高的是我姐姐，叫大美；矮的叫小真，是我妹妹，那是我弟弟叫二中，我家有六個人。
高貴:	錢太太，錢先生好！小真、大美、二中，你們好！

錢太太： 大生告訴我們，他有個好朋友，叫高貴，人很好，也很好看，我們大家都想認識認識你呢。請坐，請喝茶，吃點兒糖，別客氣。

高貴： 錢太太，您太客氣了。

大美： 小高，你不認識我了？我賣給你一張桌子，兩把椅子……。

高貴： 哦，你是商店的那位女同志啊！真對不起，我不知道您是小錢的姐姐！

錢大生： 那，沒什麼。

高貴： 小真小姐也工作嗎？

小真： 我不工作，我是學生。

高貴： 啊，我知道了。

錢太太： 你家的人都好嗎？

高貴： 都好！

錢太太： 你有兄弟姐妹嗎？

高貴： 沒有，我父母只有我一個孩子。所以，我的父母很想我。

小真： 你有愛人嗎？

錢大生： 小高，這是我們的說法，"愛人"的意思，不是女朋友，也不是男朋友，是問你有沒有太太？

高貴： 我沒有。

二中： 哥哥！你認識好些女孩子，我看你給小高介紹一個女朋友吧。

高貴： （笑）我知道，中國的說法叫"介紹對象"。

錢大生： 對，我們要給你介紹一個對象！

高貴： （笑）那，那太好了！

III.　　Chinese Character Version--Simplified Form：

看 朋 友

钱大生： 啊！小高，请进，请进！

钱太太： 欢迎，欢迎！

钱大生： 高贵，我给你介绍介绍，这是我妈妈，这是我爸爸。这位
高的是我姐姐，叫大美；矮的叫小真，是我妹妹，那是我
弟弟叫二中，我家有六个人。

高贵： 钱太太，钱先生好！小真、大美、二中，你们好！

钱太太： 大生告诉我们，他有个好朋友，叫高贵，人很好，也很好
看，我们大家都想认识认识你呢。请坐，请喝茶，吃点儿
糖，别客气。

高贵： 钱太太，您太客气了。

大美： 小高，你不认识我了？我卖给你一张桌子，两把椅子
……。

高贵： 哦，你是商店的那位女同志啊！真对不起，我不知道您
是小钱的姐姐！

钱大生： 那，没什么。

高贵： 小真小姐也工作吗？

小真： 我不工作，我是学生。

高贵： 啊，我知道了。

钱太太： 你家的人都好吗？

高贵： 都好！

钱太太： 你有兄弟姐妹吗？

高贵： 没有，我父母只有我一个孩子。所以，我的父母很想我。

小真： 你有爱人吗？

钱大生： 小高，这是我们的说法，"爱人"的意思，不是女朋友，也
不是男朋友，是问你有没有太太？

高贵： 我没有。

二中： 哥哥！你认识好些女孩子，我看你给小高介绍一个女朋
友吧。

84

高贵：　　　（笑）我知道，中国的说法叫"介绍对象"。

钱大生：　对，我们要给你介绍一个对象！

高贵：　　　（笑）那，那太好了！

PART II.　　VOCABULARY--SHĒNGCÍ 生詞

SPECIFIERS-NUMBERS (SP-NU)：　As a number **xiē** 些 indicates an unspecified small quantity. It can also be used as a numerical measure. When **xiē** is used as a number, the measure word is optional, but any number with definite quantity can not be used immediately after **xiē**. For instance, the phrase, "these seven children" should be **zhèi qī ge háizi**, not **zhèixiē háizi**, since it clearly specified the quantity, namely **qī**. **Zhèixiē qī ge háizi** is not correct.

這些	这些	zhèixiē	these
那些		nàxiē	those
哪些		něixiē	which ones?

Zhèixiē dōngxi hǎokàn, nàxiē piányi. Nǐ yào něixiē?

這些東西好看，那些便宜。你要哪些？

(These few things are good-looking, but those are inexpensive. Which ones do you want?)

NUMBER-MEASURES (NU-M)：　This is another group of Chinese numbers with indefinite quantity. **Xiē** 些 is a numerical measure here. It may be optionally followed by another measure word. As a measure, **diǎnr** 點兒 can not precede another measure.

一些		yìxiē	some, little, a few, several (see note)

Wǒ yào yìxiē táng.

我要一些糖。

(I need some sugar.)

（一）點兒	（一）点儿	(yì)diǎnr	a little, some (for things

that are not countable)

Qǐng hē yìdiǎnr chá.

請喝一點兒茶.

(Please have some tea.)

好些		hǎoxiē	quite a few, a lot

Tā gěi wǒ jièshao le hǎoxiē péngyou.

她給我介紹了好些朋友。

(She introduced a lot of friends to me.)

NOUNS (N):

父親	父親	fùqīn	father
母親	母親	mǔqīn	mother
爸(爸)		bà(ba)	dad
媽(媽)	妈妈	mā(ma)	mom
姐姐		jiějie	elder sister
妹妹		mèimei	younger sister
姐妹		jiěmèi	sisters
兄弟		xiōngdì	brothers
哥哥		gēge	elder brother
弟弟		dìdi	younger brother
兒子	儿子	érzi	son
女兒	女儿	nǚér	daughter
家		jiā	family; home; household (M: gè 個)
同志		tóngzhì	comrade
先生		xiānsheng	Mr.; teacher; husband (All three meanings are used in Taiwan, but in PRC, **xiānsheng** is used when talking with foreigners to mean Mr.; the other meanings are rarely used.)
太太		tàitai	wife; Mrs.; (married) woman (it is only popular in Taiwan

			and in overseas Chinese societies outside of PRC)
			Tāde tàitai yǒu yí ge hěn hǎo de gōngzuò.
			他的太太有一個很好的工作。
			(His wife has a very good job.)
夫人		fūrén	Madam，(married) woman (used in PRC)
			Qián fūrén yǒu liǎng ge háizi, yí ge nánde, yí ge nǚde.
			錢夫人有兩個孩子，一個男的，一個女的。
			(Madam Qian has two children, one boy and one girl.)
愛人	爱人	àirén	spouse; beloved (used in PRC for husband or wife); lover
			Wǒ àirén shì lǎoshī, tā yǒu hǎoxiē xuésheng.
			我愛人是老師，他（她）有好些學生。
			(My spouse (husband/wife) is a teacher, he/she has many students.)
小姐		xiǎojie	Miss; young lady, (unmarried) woman
			Wáng Xiǎojie, nín yǒu jǐ ge gēge?
			王小姐，您有幾個哥哥？
			(Miss Wang, how many elder brothers do you have?)
大人		dàrén	grown person, adult (M：**gè** 個, **wèi** 位)
小孩兒 小孩子	小孩儿	xiǎoháir xiǎoháizi	little child, children (M：**gè** 個) (same as above)
孩子		háizi	child, children (M：**gè** 個)
男—		(BF) nán—	male
女—		(BF) nǚ—	female
男的		nánde	man, male

女的		nǚde	woman, female
朋友		péngyou	friend (M：**wèi** 位，**gè** 個)

Tāde nánpéngyou, nǐ rènshi ma?

她的男朋友，你認識嗎？

(Do you know her boyfriend personally?)

大家		dàjiā	everybody

Nǐmen dàjiā dōu dǒng budǒng zhège wèntí?

你們大家都懂不懂這個問題？

(Do you all understand this question?)

糖		táng	sugar, candy (M：**kuài** 塊)

Nín hē chá, yào táng buyào?

您喝茶，要糖不要？

(Would you care to have some sugar in your tea?)

對象	对象	duìxiàng	partner in marriage (in PRC) (lit., target, object)

Lǎo Zhāng bùxiǎo le, tā děi zhǎo ge duìxiàng.

老張不小了，他得找個對象。

(Old Zhang is not young any more. He ought to find a partner to marry.)

有的		yǒude	some of (shows a portion of a whole—see pattern)
有人		yǒurén	some people (abbrev. of **yǒude rén**)
有些		yǒuxiē	some of (see pattern)
工作		gōngzuò (N/FV)	work, job (verb：**zuò** 做；M：**jiàn** 件，**gè** 個)

Yǒu hěn duō rén méiyǒu gōngzuo.

有很多人没有工作。

(There are many people who are out of jobs.)

Nǐ bàba zuò shénme gōngzuò?

你爸爸做什么工作？

(What is your father's occupation?)

说法	说法	shuōfa	way of speaking (lit., speaking method; M: gè 個)
想法		xiǎngfa	way of thinking, viewpoint
看法		kànfa	way of thinking, viewpoint

Nínde kànfa hěn duì.

您的看法很對。

(Your way of thinking is correct.)

ADVERB (A):

| 太 | | tài | too, excessively, too much |

Nèige gōngzuò tài bùhǎo zuò le.

那個工作太不好做了。

(That job is too difficult to do.)

Zhōngguó fàn tài hǎo chī le.

中國飯太好吃了。

(Chinese food is absolutely delicious.)

STATIVE VERVS (SV):

| 客氣 | 客气 | kèqi | be polite, standing on ceremony |

Zhāngjiā tài kèqi le.

張家太客氣了。

(The Zhang family is really courteous.)

Qǐngzuò, qǐng hēchá, bié kèqi.

請坐,請喝茶,別客氣。

(Please sit down, have some tea, please don't be ceremonious.)

| 矮 | | ǎi | short, low |

Gāo Guì gāo, wǒ ǎi.

高貴高,我矮。

(Gao Gui is tall, I'm short.)

FUNCTIVE VERBS (FV):

有	yǒu	(impersonal) there is, there are (see pattern)

Yǒurén zhǐ xǐhuan wánr, bù xǐhuan gōngzuò.

有人只喜歡玩兒，不喜歡工作。

(There are some people who like to play, but don't like to work.)

沒有	méiyǒu	(impersonal) there isn't, there aren't (see pattern)

Méiyǒu rén bùdǒng tāde yìsi.

(see pattern)

沒有人不懂他的意思。

(There is no one who doesn't understand his idea. / Everyone understands his idea)

沒(有)—FV	méi(yǒu) —FV	didn't—FV (see pattern)

Tā méi(yǒu) gěi wǒ jièshao tāde nǚpéngyou.

他沒(有)給我介紹他的女朋友。

(He didn't introduce his girlfriend to me.)

叫	jiào	call; ask; allow, let (see pattern)

Fùqīn bújiào wǒ zuò nèige gōngzuò.

父親不叫我做那個工作。

(My father won't let me take that job.)

作(做)	zuò	do, make; be engaged in

Tā zuò shénme gōngzuò?

他做什麼工作？

(What is his occupation?)

Wǒ bú huì zuò fàn.

我不會做飯。

(I don't know how to cook.)

| 認識 | 认识 | rènshi | know, recognize; be acquainted with |

Nèiwèi xiǎojie, wǒ bú rènshi.

那位小姐，我不認識。

(I am not acquainted with that young lady.)

| 介紹 | 介绍 | jièshao | introduce |
| 給…介紹 | 给…介绍 | gěi...jièshao | introduce...to... (see note) |

Wǒ gěi nǐmen jièshao jièshao.

我給你們介紹介紹。

(Let me introduce you to each other.)

Wǒ méiyǒu péngyou, qǐng nín jièshao jǐge.

我没有朋友，請您介紹幾個。

(I have no friends, please introduce some to me.)

| 玩(兒) | 玩(儿) | wánr | to play |

Xiǎoháir dōu xǐhuan wánr.

小孩兒都喜歡玩兒。

(All the children like to play.)

PARTICLE(P):

| 了 | | le | (In this lesson le is used as a verb suffix which stresses the completion of an action in the past; see pattern and note.) |

INTERJECTION (I):

| 哎呀 | | āiyā | My goodness! |

EXPRESSIONS (EX):

請進	请进	Qǐng jìn.	Please come in.
請坐	请坐	Qǐng zuò.	Please sit down.
請喝茶	请喝茶	Qǐng hēchá.	Please have some tea.
請吃糖	请吃糖	Qǐng chītáng.	Have some candy, please.
歡迎	欢迎	Huānyíng!	Welcome!
沒什麼	没什么	Méishénme.	It's nothing!

PART III. A LIST OF CHARACTERS REQUIRED
TO BE REPRODUCED FROM MEMORY

些 點 父 母 親 爸 媽 姐 妹 哥 弟 兄 男 女 孩 家
夫 朋 友 糖 工 作 做 法 太 客 氣 認 識 介 紹 了
先

PART IV. SENTENCE PATTERNS

6.1. **Yǒu** 有 with an Indeterminate Subject: This structure forms sentences that show the existence or non-existence of something. **Yǒu** 有 or **méiyǒu** 没有 are equivalent to the English " there is, there are" or "there isn't, there aren't. " This structure occurs either in a sentence with an impersonal predicate, such as **yǒu yún** 有雲 (it is cloudy) or in a sentence which has a place or time expression as the subject, which can be understood or explicitly stated. This lesson focuses on topic-comment type of sentences in which both time and place are understood.

Pattern: Topic   Comment

(Yǒu/Méiyǒu)   N   SV   O.

FV   O

Ex 1: **Yǒurén** hěn'ài háizi.

92

有人很愛孩子。

(There are some people who love children dearly.)

Ex 2: **Méiyǒu** dōngxi piányi.

沒有東西便宜。

(There is nothing that is cheap.)

6.2. Double Negative with **Méiyǒu** 没有： Using "double negatives" to produce a strong positive voice is an effective and popular device to stress one's opinion. A typical " double-negative" sentence contains **méiyǒu** plus a negative verb.

Pattern: **méiyǒu** N neg. V (O).

Ex 1: **Méiyǒu** rén **bù** xǐhuan háizi.

没有人不喜歡孩子。

(There is no one who doesn't like children.)

Ex 2: **Méiyǒu** dōngxi **bú** guì.

没有東西不貴。

(There is nothing that isn't expensive. / Everything is expensive.)

6.3. Functive Verbs with **Le** 了 or **Méiyǒu** 没有： The particle le 了, here, serves as a verb suffix in a simple sentence to indicate the completion of an action, which means the action was completed before the speaker's reference to it. This structure consisting of "FV-le" may be considered the equivalent of the past tense in English. However, the object in the sentence must be modified either by a combination " number-measure" or another modifier. Without modification the pattern "S FV-le O" only becomes a clause, not a completed sentence.

Pattern: S FV-le Mod. O.

Ex 1: Tā mǎile bùshǎo dōngxi.

她買了不少東西。

(She bought quite a few things.)

Ex 2: Tā gěi wǒ jièshaole hǎo jǐ ge péngyou.

他給我介紹了好幾個朋友。

(He introduced many friends to me.)

In negative case, **yǒu** 有 may replace the particle le 了, and in this case, inserting yǒu between méi 没 and the main verb is optional. The main verb, by the way, is a functive verb. The modifier of the object is not required for this to be a completed sentence in the negative case.

Pattern: S méi(yǒu) FV (Mod.) O.

Ex：Wǒmen dōu **méi**(yǒu) huà hěnduō huàr.

我們都没(有)畫很多畫兒。

(None of us does a lot of paintings.)

6.4. The Structure of "**Tài** 太 **SV Le** 了"：　This structure may be used for the purpose of exaggeration. It is also a "topic-comment" type of sentence.

Pattern：Topic　　　　Comment.

(**tài**　SV　**le**).

Ex 1：Nínde háizi tài hǎo kàn le.

您的孩子太好看了。

(Your child is extremely beautiful.)

Ex 2：Zuò nèige gōngzuò, tài méi yìsi le.

做那個工作，太没意思了。

(It is extremely boring to do that job.)

6.5. The Whole Stands Before the Part：　In a sentence that describes the various compo-nents of an aggregation, a collective or plural noun referring to the whole begins the sentence, then the parts follow. Instead of saying as in English, "Half of those ten children are boys," the Chinese way is, "As for the ten children, half of them are boys."

Pattern 1：Whole, yǒude/yǒuxiē/yǒurén...

yǒude/yǒuxiē/yǒurén...

Ex：Huàr, yǒude shì wǒde, yǒude shì wǒ péngyoude.

畫兒，有的是我的，有的是我朋友的。

(Some of the paintings are mine, others belong to a friend of mine.)

Pattern 2：Whole, (yǒu) NU1-M..., (yǒu) NU2-N...

Ex：Wǒ zhèixiē péngyou, sān wèi shì Fǎguórén, jiǔ wèi shì Rìběnrén.

我這些朋友，三位是法國人，九位是日本人。

(Three of these friends of mine are Frenchmen, the other nine are Japanese.)

Pattern 3：Whole, SP1-NU1-M..., SP2—NU2—M...

Ex：Tāde shū, zhèi jǐ běn gěi wǒ, nà jǐ běn gěi nǐ.

他的書，這幾本給我，那幾本給你。

(He'll give these few books of his to me, and those few to you.)

Pattern 4: Whole, Noun Phrase 1... Noun Phrase 2...

    Ex 1: Háizi, nánde, tā xǐhuan, nǚde, tā bùxǐhuan.

        孩子，男的，他喜歡，女的，他不喜歡。

        (As for the children, he likes the boys not the girls.)

    Ex 2: Shū, guìde duō, piányide shǎo.

        書，貴的多，便宜的少。

        (The expensive books are numerous, but the inexpensive ones are few.)

The expression bùdōu 不都 (not all) may be applied here, and it can be combined with the above mentioned parts to express "some of," for example:

    Ex 1: Wàiguóhuà, wǒ bùdōu huì shuō, yǒude wǒ huì, yǒude wǒ búhuì.

        外國話，我不都會說，有的我會，有的我不會。

        (Of all the foreign languages, I can speak some, but not the others.)

    Ex 2: Qián bùdōu shì tāde, yǒude shì tā tàitaide.

        錢不都是他的，有的是他太太的。

        (All the money doesn't belong to him, some of it belongs to his wife.)

6.6.   The Usages of Duō 多 When It Means "Plus":   Duō 多 has two functions:

A.   Duō is used as "plus some" in the pattern "NU-duō-M-N." When the number is a figure of two or more digits, duō indicates that the actual amount exceeds the "number" stated in the sentence.

Pattern: "NU—duō—M—N"

    Ex 1: shí duō běn shū (same as "shíjǐ běn shū")

        十多本書

        (more than ten volumes of books)

    Ex 2: sānshí duō wèi péngyou

        三十多位朋友

        (over thirty friends)

    Ex 3: èrbǎi duō ge xuéshēng

        二百多個學生

        (over two hundred students)

    Ex 4: wǔqiān duō kuài qián

        五千多塊錢

        (over five thousand dollars)

6.7.   The Usages of Jiào 叫:

A.   To inquire about a name:

Pattern: <u>Noun   A   **jiào**   Noun   B.</u>

    1. Of a person:

    Ex: Nǐ jiào shénme míngzi?

        你叫什么名字？

        （What is your name?）

Here, **míngzi** may refer either to the given name or the full name, depending on the context.

    2. Of things:

    Ex: Zhèige dōngxi jiào shénme (míngzi)?

        這個東西叫什么（名字）？

        （What is this called?）

B.   To address people by their titles:

Pattern: Subject **jiào** Object in a Position.

       <u>Noun A **jiào** Noun B, Title.</u>

Noun B is the referent of the title and it precedes the "title."

    Ex: Wǒ jiào tā lǎoshī.

        我叫他老師。

        （I call him teacher.）

C.   To make causative sentences: (see note)

    1.   To ask for a favor: **Jiào** 叫 has similar functions as **qǐng** 請 but with a different voice. It can show difference in rank, in a situation in life (see Ex 2). **Jiào** can also be a polite form of speech, when a subordinate, or younger person, is imploring the wishes of his superior (see Ex 1.)

Pattern: <u>S   **jiào**   O.</u>

       <u>(S   V   O).</u>

    Ex 1: Nín jiào wǒ mǎi shénme dōngxi?

        您叫我買什么東西？

        （What are you asking me to buy?）

    Ex 2: Fùqin jiào érzi gěi tā yí fènr bào.

        父親叫兒子給他一份兒報。

        （Father asked the son to hand a newspaper to him.）

    2.   To grant or deny permission: **Jiào** (叫) can have the meaning of "allow" with a very strong or restricted voice.

Pattern: <u>S   **jiào**   O.</u>

       <u>(S   V   O).</u>

Ex 1: Mǔqin jiào háizi chī nàxiē táng.

母親叫孩子吃那些糖。

(Mother allows the child to eat those candies.)

Ex 2: Lǎoshī bújiào wǒ shuō wàiguóhuà.

老師不叫我說外國話。

(The teacher doesn't allow me to speak any foreign languages.)

PART V.   GRAMMAR NOTES AND OTHERS

1. In this country, smokers are responsible for furnishing their own cigarettes. It is tradition in Chinese society that the host, in order to show hospitality, offers not only tea to guests, but also candy to women and children and cigarettes to men and even to some women if they smoke. Prior to the introduction of cigarettes, Chinese offered pipes or water-pipes to guests. It seems, despite health education campaigns to promote the contrary, smoking is still quite common in China.

2. More information about Chinese way of addressing one another and of inquiring about one's name: Nín guìxìng? The traditional courteous form of making direct inquisitions is still quite common in both the Mainland and Taiwan. To replay, one could simply say, Wǒ xìng--, Wǒde míngzi jiào/shì--. The courtesy word guì 貴 is not used. Similarly, in stating one's nationality guìguó 貴國 should not be included. Since Chinese people have only limited surnames, but unlimited given names, the most prevalent way to address someone with affection is to put xiǎo 小 (for younger, or comparatively younger persons) or lǎo 老 (for older ones to show respect for their age, not to insult the wrinkled appearance) in front of the surname, instead of calling that person by the given name. For instance, the name Xiǎo Gāo 小高 represents a young man or woman whose surname is Gāo, and Lǎo Lǐ 老李 is an older man or woman (the women in the PRC may not be in favor of being called "lǎo—," but apparently are not offended by it). The use of the word xiǎo or lǎo is common in the PRC in addressing colleagues and peers, since the expressions such as xiānsheng, tàitai and xiǎojie were the titles used in the ruling class during the Old China, and are symbols of bourgeois ideology. The word tóngzhì alone without the surname is just like saying "hello" or "hey, you." It is used to call, or refer to, a person whose identity is unknown. Calling someone as Zhāng tóngzhì, Wáng tóngzhì is rather too formal and too bureaucratic.

In Taiwan, **Xiǎo—** and **Lǎo—** have rather different usage. They are quite popular on school campuses or between very close friends. But one can never call an older woman **Lǎo—** (although the word **lǎo tàitai**, old lady, is well-received and respectful). **Xiānsheng, lǎo xiānsheng, tàitai, lǎo tàitai** and **xiǎojie** are the appropriate phrases to use in calling someone with whom you do not have an intimate acquaintance. For a career woman, the way to address her is **xiǎojie** (except if she is a teacher, then call her **lǎoshī**), even if she is married with children, or no longer young.

3. "How old are you?" "Are you married?" "Do you have any children?" and "How much do you earn?" All these questions are commonly used to convey interest and care. As such, they are not construed as invasions of privacy. To help people have a happy life and a family is everybody's business, and this begins with a show of strong interest in other people's personal life. Even now an eligible man and woman will receive enthusiastic match-making efforts from colleagues, relatives and neighbors.

4. Using Reduplicated Forms for Emphasis: Some monosyllabic nouns can appear in a reduplicated form to mean "every," or "each." They are used as sentence subjects only, and are followed by the totalizer **dōu**. **Rénrén dōu** is one of the typical examples. A disyllabic verb can be repeated for emphasis only in its bound form. Neither **le** 了 nor **yī** 一 may be inserted. If the functive verb is a transitive verb, its object should be transposed to the beginning of the sentence so that the functive verb may appear in reduplicated form. For instance, **Wǒ yào gěi tā jièshao nèige nǚpéngyou.** (I'm going to introduce that girlfriend to him.) To stress **jièshao** 介紹, the sentence is changed into **Nèige nǚpéngyou, wǒ yào gěi tā jièshao jièshao.**

5. To Differentiate **Qǐng** 請 and **jiào** 叫: Both **qǐng** 請 and **jiào** 叫 may be interpreted as "ask to do a favor." But how do you use them properly? It is simply a matter of courtesy. When you ask someone else to do something for you, it is always appropriate to use the word **qǐng**. On the other hand, **jiào** is the better word when you are asked if there is something you can do for someone else.

6. Particle Le: This lesson introduced **le** 了 as a verb suffix to indicate completion of an action, and **tài SV le** 太 SV 了 as a sentence structure for exaggeration. **Le** is one of the most difficult Chinese particle to master. Many consider **le** to show past tense; however, this may not necessarily be true since time-when expressions are crucial in conveying

whether an action happens in the past, present or future. The verb suffix **le** may not be the sole factor. Thus, it would be better to say that the verb suffix **le** is a marker of perfection. **Le** can also be found at the end of a sentence as a modal particle. More information about the usages of **le** will be mentioned in the next few lessons.

7. "Some" and "Any": The English word "some" is used in two different senses-- stressed or unstressed.

a. In Chinese, the unstressed English "some," indicating an indefinite amount, is understood, and so is the English word "any" which is used instead of "some" in negative sentences.

Do you want some?	Nǐ yào buyào?
Don't you want any?	Nǐ búyào ma?
I don't have any.	Wǒ méiyǒu.
I'm not buying any books.	Wǒ bùmǎi shū.

The amount which is expressed by the structure **jǐ—M** is countable, while an amount represented by the expression **yìdiǎnr** is not countable and can not be divided into units.

I have some money.	Wǒ yǒu yìdiǎnr qián.
She has some paintings.	Tā yǒu jǐzhāng huàr.
Is this little bit enough?	Zhèi (yī)diǎnr gòu bugòu?

b. The stressed "some" usually indicates a part of a larger whole. Since the whole must stand before the part, the Chinese would say, in effect, "as for these, some are good" rather than "some of these are good."

Some of these books are yours, some are mine.

(Zhèixiē shū, yǒude shì nǐde, yǒude shì wǒde.)

Some pictorials I read often, others I don't.

(Yǒude huàbào wǒ cháng kàn, yǒude wǒ búkàn.)

c. Note that while **jǐ—M** and **yìdiǎnr** may stand either before or after the verb, "**yǒude**" can not stand after the verb. Hence, it must take the topic position at the beginning of the sentence, e.g., I like some people. (Yǒude rén, wǒ xǐhuan).

8. Related chapters in *Essential Grammar for Modern Chinese* are Chapter VII——Determinatives and Measures; Chapter VIII——The Functive Verb **yǒu** 有; Chapter X——The Usages of **Le**, pp. 133—136; and Chapter XVIII——Placing Emphasis Within a Sentence, pp. 259—260.

PART VI.   TRANSLATION OF THE TEXT

Visiting a Friend

Qian Dasheng: Hello, Xiao Gao. Come in, please.

Mrs. Qian: Welcome, welcome!

Qian Dasheng: Gao Gui, let me introduce you. This is my mother, and this is my father. The tall one is Damei, my elder sister, and the short one is Xiaozhen, my younger sister. That's Erzhong, my younger brother. We have six members in our family.

Gao Gui: How do you do, Mr. and Mrs. Qian? How are you, Xiaozhen, Damei and Erzhong?

Mrs. Qian: Dasheng has told us that he has a good friend called Gao Gui who is a nice and handsome young man. We all want to get to know you. Sit down, please. Have some tea and sweets. Make yourself at home.

Gao Gui: You are so kind, Mrs. Qian.

Damei: Don't you recognize me, Xiao Gao? I sold you a table and two chairs...

Gao Gui: Oh, you are the lady comrade of the shop. I didn't know you were Xiao Qian's sister.

Qian Dasheng: That's no problem.

Gao Gui: Does Miss Xiaozhen also have a job?

Xiaozhen: I don't work. I'm a student now.

Gao Gui: Oh, I see.

Mrs. Qian: How is your family?

Gao Gui: They're all fine.

Mrs. Qian: Do you have any brothers and sisters?

Gao Gui: No. I'm my parents' only child, therefore,

	they miss me very much.
Mrs. Qian:	Do you have an "**àirén**"?
Qian Dasheng:	Xiao Gao, "airen" is our way of saying. It doesn't mean girlfriend and boyfriend. (My mother) was asking you whether you have a wife.
Gao Gui:	No, I haven't.
Erzhong:	Elder brother, you know a lot of girls, why don't you introduce a girlfriend for Xiao Gao?
Gao Gui:	(laughing) I know. The Chinese say: "Introduce a marriage partner."
Qian Dasheng:	Right. I'm going to introduce a girlfriend for you.
Gao Gui:	(laughing) Oh, that sounds great!

Lesson 7

Modal Particles: **Le**, **Ne** and **Bǎ**
and Time Elements

PART I.   TEXT

Story: **Yí Ge Xiǎo Gùshi**--A Short Story

I.   *Pinyin* Romanization:

Yǒu yì tiān, Gāo Guì shuō:"Xiǎo Qián, nǐ hěn ài tīng gùshi ba! Cóngqián wǒde Zhōngwén búdà hǎo, biéren shuō gùshi, wǒ yě bù dǒng. Xiànzài, wǒde Zhōngwén hǎo yìdiǎnr le. Gāngcái, wǒ rènshile yí ge péngyou, tā gěi wǒ shuōle yí ge gùshi, xiànzài, wǒ zài shuōgěi nǐ tīngting, nǐ kàn yǒu meiyǒu yìsi?"

Cóngqián, yǒu yí ge shāngrén, xìng Wén. Wénjiā yǒu yí ge xiǎo shāngdiàn, mài kāfēi, diǎnxin, mǎide rén hěnduō, shēngyi   hěn   hǎo. Wén xiānsheng, Wén tàitai méiyǒu nǚér, zhǐyǒu yí ge érzi jiào Dànán. Dànán tā fēicháng lǎn, bù kěn xuéxí, yě bú ài zuò shì, měitiān zhǐ zhīdao wánr. Tā chángcháng xiǎng: "Wǒ fùqīnde diǎnxindiàn hěn dà, shēngyi yě hěn hǎo, wǒ jiāde qián gòu duōde, wǒ méiyǒu xiōngdì jiěmèi, jiānglái fùmǔ de qián dōu shì wǒde, wǒ wèishénme yào xuéxí, gōngzuò ne? Fùqīn lǎo jiào wǒ xué zuò shēngyi, zhēn jiào wǒ bù shūfu. Wǒ búbì tīng tāde huà, háishi tiàotiao wǔ, chàngchang gēr, chīchi wánwanr ba! Xiànzài wǒde fùmǔ hái bù lǎo, shìqing tāmen kěyǐ zuò, yǐhòu tāmen lǎo le, wǒ zài xiǎng zhǎo shéi gěi wǒ zuò shì ba!"

Zhè yì tiān, tāde mǔqīn gàosu tā:" Nǐ fùqīn bù shūfu, bùnéng zài gōngzuò le. wǒmen shēngyi hěn máng, rén bú gòu, nǐ yě děi xuéxí zuò shì le. " Mǔqīn gàosu tā, zuò shēngyi yào huì shuōhuà, yào kèqi, biéren wèn nǐ kāfēi hǎo hē ma? Diǎnxin hǎo chī ma? Nǐ dōu yào shuō:" Hǎo! Wǒ měitiān dōu chī zhèixiē dōngxi."

    Xiànzài Dànán gōngzuòle. Yǒu yì tiān, yǒu yí wèi xiǎojie   mǎi dōngxi, tā
wèn:"Wǒ hěn kě, yě hěn è, xiǎng hē diǎnr kāfēi, chī diǎnr diǎnxin." Dànán
shuō:"Hǎo, nín qǐng zuò ba!" Nàwei xiǎojie shuō:"Yǐqián, wǒ chángcháng
mǎi nǐmen   de diǎnxin, nǐmende diǎnxin zhēn hǎo, xiànzài hái mài ma?"
Dànán shuō:"Mài a, nǐ kàn, zhèikuài diǎnxin hěn hǎochī!" Xiǎojie wèn tā:" Nǐ
wèishénme shuō zhèikuài hǎochī ne?" Dànán shuō:" Zhèikuài wǒ chīle yìdiǎnr,
suǒyǐ wǒ shuō hǎochī. Biéde, wǒ bù zhīdao, yīnwèi wǒ hái méi chī ne, wǒ
xiànzài bǎo le."

II.   Chinese Character Version——Regular Form:

一 個 小 故 事

　　有一天,高貴說:"小錢,你很愛聽故事吧! 從前我的中文不大
好,別人說故事,我也不懂。現在,我的中文好一點兒了。剛才,我
認識了一個朋友,他給我說了一個故事,現在,我再說給你聽聽,你
看有沒有意思?"

　　從前,有一個商人,姓文。文家有一個小商店,賣咖啡,點心,
買的人很多,生意很 好。文先生、文太太沒有女兒,只有一個兒
子叫大男。大男他非常懶,不肯學習,也不愛做事,每天只知道玩
兒。他常常想:"我父親的點心店很大,生意也很好,我家的錢够多
的,我沒有兄弟姐妹,將來父母的錢都是我的,我爲什麽要學習、工
作呢? 父親老叫我學做生意,真叫我不舒服。我不必聽他的話,還
是跳跳舞,唱唱歌,吃吃玩兒玩兒吧! 現在我的父母還不老,事情
他們可以做,以後他們老了,我再想找誰給我做事吧!"

　　這一天,他的母親告訴他:" 你父親不舒服,不能再工作了。
我們生意很忙,人不够,你也得學習做事了。"母親告訴他,做生意

要會说話，要客氣，別人問你咖啡好喝嗎？點心好吃嗎？你都要说：
"好！我每天都吃這些東西。"

現在大男工作了。有一天，有一位小姐　買東西，她問："我很
渴，也很餓，想喝點兒咖啡，吃點兒點心。"大男说："好，您請坐
吧！"那位小姐说："以前，我常常買你們　　的點心，你們的點心真
好，現在還賣嗎？"大男说："賣啊，你看，這塊點心很好吃！"小姐
問他："你爲什麼说這塊好吃呢？"大男说："這塊我吃了一點兒，所
以我说好吃。別的，我不知道，因爲我還没吃呢，我現在飽了。"

III.　　Chinese Character Version——Simplified Form：

一 个 小 故 事

有一天，高贵说："小钱，你很爱听故事吧！从前我的中文不大
好，别人说故事，我也不懂。现在，我的中文好一点儿了。刚才，我
认识了一个朋友，他给我说了一个故事，现在，我再说给你听听，你
看有没有意思？"

从前，有一个商人，姓文。文家有一个小商店，卖咖啡，点心，
买的人很多；生意　很　好。文先生、文太太没有女儿，只有一个儿
子叫大男。大男他非常懒，不肯学习，也不爱做事，每天只知道玩
儿。他常常想："我父亲的点心店很大，生意也很好，我家的钱够多
的，我没有兄弟姐妹，将来父母的钱都是我的，我为什么要学习、工
作呢？父亲老叫我学做生意，真叫我不舒服。我不必听他的话，还
是跳跳舞，唱唱歌，吃吃玩儿玩儿吧！现在我的父母还不老，事情
他们可以做，以后他们老了，我再想找谁给我做事吧！"

这一天，他的母亲告诉他："你父亲不舒服，不能再工作了。
我们生意很忙，人不够，你也得学习做事了。"母亲告诉他，做生意

104

要会说话,要客气,别人问你咖啡好喝吗?点心好吃吗? 你都要说:
"好! 我每天都吃这些东西。"

现在大男工作了。有一天,有一位小姐　买东西,她问:"我很渴,也很饿,想喝点儿咖啡,吃点儿点心。"大男说:"好,您请坐吧!"那位小姐说:"以前,我常常买你们　　的点心,你们的点心真好,现在还卖吗?"大男说:"卖啊,你看,这块点心很好吃!"小姐问他:"你为什么说这块好吃呢?"大男说:"这块我吃了一点儿,所以我说好吃。别的,我不知道,因为我还没吃呢,我现在饱了。"

PART II.　　VOCABULARY——SHĒNGCÍ　生詞

PRONOUNS (PN):

每		měi (BF)	every, each (a demonstrative pronoun; when **měi** is used as a subjective modifier to a noun, **dōu** is normally used.) Nàxiē táng, měige háizi dōu kěyǐ chī yí kuàir. 那些糖,每個孩子都可以吃一塊(兒)。 (Each child can have a piece of those candies.)

TIME-WHEN EXPRESSIONS (TW/N/MA):　Nouns which also function as movable adverbs. (see note.)

從前	从前	cóngqián	previously, formerly, once, long time ago Tā cóngqián hěn lǎn, (kěshì) xiànzài ài gōngzuò le. 他從前很懶,(可是)現在愛工作了。

(Formerly he was very lazy, now
he likes to work.)

現在	現在	xiànzài	present, now, currently

Měiguó xiànzài yǒu bùshǎo
rén xué Zhōngwén.

美國現在有不少人學中文。

(Currently there are quite a few
people learning Chinese in the
United States.)

每天	měitiān	every day

Mětiān nǐ dōu gōngzuò ma?

每天你都工作嗎？

(Do you work everyday?)

NOUNS(N):

事(情)		shì (qing)	matter, affair, thing
事(兒)	事(儿)	shìr	matter, affair; job (M：**jiàn** 件，**gè** 個)

Wǒ yǒu shìr yào gàosu nín.

我有事兒要告訴告訴您。

(I have something that I'd like
to tell you.)

生意	shēngyi	business (M：**gè** 個)

Xiànzài shēngyi hěn bùhǎo zuò.

現在生意很不好做。

(Now it is difficult to run a
business)

買賣	买卖	mǎimai	business (M：**gè** 個)

Nàge jiǔdiàn de mǎimai búdà hǎo.

那個酒店的買賣不大好。

(The business is quite slow at
that liquor store.)

故事	gùshi	story, tale (M：**gè** 個)

Qǐng nín shuō yí ge gùshi, kěyǐ ba.

請您説一個故事，可以吧。

(Please tell us a story, OK？)

歌		gē(r)	song（M：gè 個）

Nín ài chàng shénme gēr?

您愛唱什么歌？

(What sort of songs do you like to sing?)

點心	点心	diǎnxin	pastry, light refreshment, snack（M：kuài 塊）
茶		chá	tea
酒		jiǔ	liquor, wine
水		shuǐ	water
汽水		qìshuǐ	carbonated drink, soft drink, soda
咖啡		kāfēi	coffee
天		tiān	day（is also M itself）

ADVERBS (A)：

就	jiù	only, just; then (introduces subsequent action), soon (see note)

Wǒ jiù yǒu yí ge mèimei.

我就有一個妹妹。

(I have only one little sister.)

就（要）…了	jiù (yào)…le	then, immediately

Wǒmen jiùyào chī fàn le.

我們就要吃飯了。

(We are about to eat our meal.)

再	zài	again (in the future, making a suggestion or an imperative mood sentence); then (in the future; contrast yòu 又)

Qǐng zài hē yìdiǎnr chá.

請再喝一點兒茶。

(Please have some more tea.)

Zàijiàn! Wǒmen yǐhòu zài
tiàowǔ ba!

再見！我們以後再跳舞吧！

(Goodbye, we'll dance together
again another time.)

剛才	刚才	gāngcái	just now, a short while ago

(refers only to very current time)

Gāngcái nǐ shuō shénme le?

剛才你說什麼了？

(What did you say just a moment ago?)

將來	将来	jiānglái	in the future
將來…	将来…	jiānglái...	will . . . in the future
就…了	就…了	jiù. . . le	

Wǒ jiānglái jiù yǒu qián le.

我將來就有錢了。

(I'll be rich in the future.)

以前	yǐqián	before, previously

Yǐqián nǐ búdà ài tā, xiànzài ne?

以前你不大愛他，現在呢？

(You didn't love him very
much before, how about now?)

以後	以后	yǐhòu	later, afterward, hereafter

Wǒmen xiànzài xuéxí, yǐhòu
zài wánr ba.

我們現在學習，以後再玩兒吧。

(Let's study now, and play
afterward.)

有一天	yǒuyìtiān	one day

Yǒuyìtiān tā lǎo le, jiù
wàngle wǒ shì shéi le.

有一天他老了，就忘了我是誰了。

(One day when he gets really old,
he will forget who I am.)

還…呢	还…呢	hái. . . ne	still, yet (continuing or suspense; see pattern)

Tāmen hái tiàowǔ ne.

他們還跳舞呢。

(They are still dancing now.)

Wǒ hái méichī diǎnxin ne.

我還沒吃點心呢。

(I still haven't had my snacks.)

AUXILIARY VERB (AV):

肯	kěn	be willing to

Tā bùkěn shuō Zhōngguó huà.

她不肯說中國話。

(She is not willing to speak Chinese.)

FUNCTIVE VERBS (FV):

學習	学习	xuéxí	learn (a popular term in PRC)

Xiànzài hěn duō rén dōu
xuéxí Yīngyǔ.

現在很多人都學習英語。

(A lot of people are learning
English now.)

唱		chàng	sing
喝		hē	drink
跳		tiào	jump
聽	听	tīng	hear, listen

Tā bùtīng tā fùqīn de huà.

他不聽他父親的話。

(He doesn't listen to what his
father says.)

STATIVE VERBS (SV):

老	lǎo (A/SV)	always; be old

Tā lǎo shuō nàjiàn shìqing.

她老說那件事情。

(She always keeps talking about that matter.)

Rén lǎo le, hái děi gōngzuò ma?

人老了，還得工作嗎？

(Once a person is old, does he still have to work?)

懶	懒	lǎn	be lazy

Tā búshì yí ge lǎnrén, kěshi yě bú yuànyi zuò tài duō de shì.

他不是一個懶人，可是也不願意做太多的事。

(He is not a lazy guy, but he doesn't want to do too much work.)

飽	饱	bǎo	be full, satisfied of eating

Tài bǎo le, bùnéng zài chī le.

太飽了，不能再吃了。

(I am too full, I cannot eat any more.)

餓	饿	è	be hungry

Wǒ zhēn è, shéi kěyǐ gěi wǒ jǐ kuài diǎnxin?

我真餓，誰可以給我幾塊點心？

(I am really hungry, who can give me some snacks to eat?)

渴	kě	be thirsty

Wǒ kě le, xiǎng hē chá.

我渴了，想喝茶。

(I am thirsty, I want to have some tea.)

舒服	shūfu	be comfortable

Tāde jiā zhēn shūfu.

他的家真舒服。

(His house is really comfortable.)

Gāngcái tā bùshūfu le, méi chī fàn, xiànzài tā hǎo le.

剛才她不舒服了，沒吃飯，現在她好了。

(Just a while ago, she wasn't well and didn't eat, but now she is recovered.)

VERB-OBJECTS (VO):

唱歌		chàng gēr	sing (songs)
喝茶		hē chá	drink tea
喝酒		hē jiǔ	drink (wine or liquor)
喝汽水		hē qìshuǐ	drink soda
喝咖啡		hē kāfēi	drink coffee
跳舞		tiào wǔ	dance

Měiguórén dōu huì tiào wǔ ba.

美國人都會跳舞吧。

(I suppose every American knows how to dance.)

做生意		zuò shēngyi	be engaged in business
做買賣	做买卖	zuò mǎimai	be engaged in business
做飯	做饭	zuò fàn	to cook
做點心	做点心	zuò diǎnxin	bake pastry
做事		zuò shì	work; be engaged in an occupation

PARTICLES (P):

了	le	as a modal particle indicating change of status (see pattern and note)
呢	ne	as a modal particle indicating continuous action or suspense (see pattern)
吧	ba	as a modal particle indicating suggestion or probability (see pattern)

111

PART III.   A LIST OF CHARACTERS REQUIRED
TO BE REPRODUCED FROM MEMORY

每 從 前 現 在 剛 才 後 將 就 天 事 情 夏 歌 心
茶 酒 水 再 還 習 唱 喝 聽 懶 飽 餓 渴 舒 服 吧
肯

PART IV.   SENTENCE PATTERNS

7. 1.   <u>Change Status with the Modal Particle **Le** 了</u>:

A.   First let us compare the following sets of sentences, so we may find out what kind of function the modal particle le 了 can perform with respect to the subjects of each sentence:

Group 1:   Without the ending le   Group 2: With the ending le

a.   Hái zi dà.   a.   Háizi dà le.
     孩子大。   孩子大了。
     (The child is big.)   (The child has grown up.)

b.   Wǒ méiyǒu qián.   b.   Wǒ méiyǒu qián le.
     我没有錢。   我没有錢了。
     (I don't have money.)   (I have no money left.)

c.   Tā bú yuànyi chàng gēr.   c.   Tā bú yuànyi chàng gēr le.
     她不願意唱歌兒。   她不願意唱歌兒了。
     (She doesn't want to sing.)   (She doesn't want to sing any
                                               more.)

In Group 2, the ending particle le occurs at the end of every sentence. The le here does not carry any meaning itself, but its occurrence leads the sentences to imply that the condition, attitude or action of the subjects in these sentences has changed. Hence, this modal particle le is called a marker of change of status le or "change of status le. " In this usage, it describes the agent or the topic rather than the action.

The presence of le at the end of a sentence also implies that the status described by the sentence is the very opposite of a prior condition.

112

Present Status:

Ex 1: Tā búshì lǎoshī le.

她不是老師了。

(She is no longer a teacher.)

Ex 2: Tā mǎi bào le.

他買報了。

(He has bought a newspaper now.)

Implied Prior Status:

Tā shì lǎoshī.

她是老師。

(She was a teacher.)

Tā méi mǎi bào.

他没買報。

(He didn't buy a newspaper.)

B.　The Time Elements: This modal particle **le** refers to the change of the subjects' status. It does not give any indication of tenses. It is the same as the verb suffix **le**, neither of which indicates past tense. To ascertain whether something has happened in the past, present or even in the future, we must refer to "Time-When" expressions such as **yǐqián** 以前 (previously), **gāngcái** 剛才 (just a short while ago), **xiànzài** 現在 (presently), **jiānglái** 將來 (in the future), etc., or to the context if it may show the tense. Generally, if a Chinese sentence contains no Time-When expression, it may be interpreted as "at present" or "at the time when the story is unfolding." For instance: **Tā bú rènshi wǒ le.** 他不認識我了。(He doesn't recognize me any more.) However, in order to describe a change over time, a pair of related "Time-When" expressions are usually found in a sentence. Each expression is contained in a clause, and the movable adverb **kěshì** may be used as a connective to link the clauses together for emphasizing difference in time.

Ex 1: Cóngqián tā bú tiào wǔ, (kěshi) xiànzài hěn ài tiào (wǔ) le.

從前她不跳舞,(可是)現在很愛跳(舞)了。

(She didn't dance before, but now she enjoys dancing very much.)

Ex 2: Xiànzài tā shì xiǎo háizi, jiù ài wánr; jiānglái chéng dàrén le, jiù búdà ài wánr le.

現在他是小孩子,就愛玩兒;將來成大人了,就不大愛玩兒了。

(Now he is a little boy, he loves to play; but in the future, he'll grow up and won't like to play that much.)

C.　Change of status expressed by different kinds of verbs:

1.　With stative verbs:

a.　Using the construction "**tài SV le** 太 SV 了": This **le** is used as a complement of a stative verb for the purpose of exaggeration (see Lesson 6).

b.　Using the construction "SV **le**": The **le** here refers to the changes in the subject from one set of attributes to the opposite set. Moreover, since a stative verb here serves as a main verb in a sentence, and the verb does not require an object, in the structure "S SV **le**," the particle **le** has dual functions: (1) as a marker of change of status, and (2) as a marker of completion of action. For instance, a sentence such as **Háizi gāo** 孩子高 means "The child is tall," but after the modal particle le is added to the end of the statement as in **háizi gāo le** 孩子高了 the sentence can be interpreted as "The child is getting taller now." Hence, not only has the status of the child changed, but, simultaneously, the action of "growing up" is also completed up to a point. Because of this, the form of "SV **le**" may be treated as an expression which carries the same function as a functive verb does.

Pattern: <u>(MA)* S (MA) pos. /neg. SV **le**.</u>

   * MA refers to "Time-When" expression.

   Ex: Gāngcái wǒ bu shūfu **le**.

   剛才我不舒服了。

   (Just now I didn't feel very well.)

2.   With equative verbs: The sentence mainly indicates change in the status of the subject, but does not suggest any reason or action that is associated with this change.

Pattern: <u>(MA) N1 (MA) pos. / neg. EV N2 **le**.</u>

   Ex 1: **Jiānglái** nín jiù shì lǎoshī **le**.

   將來您就是老師了。

   (You will be a teacher in the future.)

   Ex 2: Xiànzài tā búshì ge shāngrén **le**.

   現在她不是個商人了。

   (Now she is no longer a business woman.)

3.   With functive verbs: The same applies to functive verbs. Since **le** may indicate that the action or occurrence starts or stops when the main verb is a functive verb, this type of sentence explains the change in the status of the agent's activation or deactivation:

Pattern: <u>(MA) S (MA) pos. /neg. FV O **le**.</u>

   Ex 1: **Gāngcái** wǒ xué Zhōngwén **le**.

   剛才我學中文了.

   (Just now I have studied Chinese.)

   Ex 2: Wǒ yǐhòu búzài hē jiǔ **le**.

   我以後不再喝酒了。

   (I won't drink any more.)

4.   With auxiliary verb:

   a. To indicate a change in state or condition:

Pattern: (MA) S (MA) pos. /neg. AV FV O · le.

Ex 1: Wǒ xiànzài kěyǐ wánr **le**.

我現在可以玩兒了。

(I can play now.)

b. Imminent action: With the assistance of an adverb, such as **jiù** 就 (soon), and/or an auxiliary verb **yào** 要 (shall, will), le can indicate the subject's intention to undertake certain courses of action. So, the status of the agent will soon be changed. This type of sentence is called "imminent action."

Pattern: (MA) S (MA) jiù pos. /neg. AV FV O le.

Ex 1: Tā yǐhòu **jiù** yào gōngzuò **le**.

她以後就要工作了。

(Soon she is going to work.)

Ex 2: Jiānglái nǐ **jiù** bú yuànyi tīng tāde huà le.

將來你就不願意聽他的話了。

(Later on, you will not want to listen to him any more.)

D. Two-clause sentences with time contrast: When a sentence contains two clauses to show a change over time, this changed status is further emphasized by the use of the modal particle le.

Pattern: MA1 S1 pos. /neg. V; (**kěshì**), MA2 S2 pos. /neg. V le.

Ex 1: **Cóngqián** tā hěn lǎn, bú zuòshì; **kěshì**, xiànzài bùlǎn **le**.

從前他很懶,不做事;可是,現在不懶了。

(He used to be very lazy, and didn't work; but now he works and is no longer lazy.)

Ex 2: Nǐ **yǐqián** méi qián, bùnéng mǎi; **jiānglái** yǒu qián le, jiù kěyǐ mǎi **le**.

你以前没錢,不能買;將來有錢了,就可以買了。

(Previously, you didn't have any money, you couldn't buy it; but in the future, when you have money, you'll be able to buy it.)

7.2. <u>Continuity or Suspension with the Construction **Hái** 還 V **ne** 呢</u>: The modal particle **ne** 呢 has several uses. One of its functions is to show the continuation of a condition or occurrence, especially when **ne** is placed in the structure **hái** V **ne**. In this pattern, if the verb is in a positive case, it shows that the state or action expressed by the verb is on-going, for example, **Tāmen hái chàng gēr ne.** 他們還唱歌呢。(They are still singing.) If the verb is in the negative case, it indicates that the desired state still has not occurred, and eventual change is being eagerly awaited, as in **Nǐ hái bùnéng hē jiǔ ne ma?** 你還不能喝酒呢嗎? (Are you still not supposed to drink?)

115

Pattern 1: With SV: <u>S **hái** pos. /neg. SV **ne**.</u>

Ex: Xiànzài dōngxi **hái** bùpiányi **ne**.

現在東西還不便宜呢。

(Now things are still expensive.)

Pattern 2: With EV: <u>N1 **hái** pos. /neg. EV N2 **ne**.</u>

Ex: Tā **hái** shì xuéshēng **ne** ma?

她還是學生呢嗎?

(Is she still a student?)

Pattern 3: With FV: <u>S **hái** neg. FV O **ne**.</u>

Ex: Zhāng tàitai **hái** méi zuò fàn **ne**.

張太太還沒做飯呢。

(Mrs. Zhang still hasn't cooked yet.)

Pattern 4: With FV yǒu: <u>S **hái** (**méi**)yǒu O **ne**.</u>

Ex: Wǒ **hái** méiyǒu gōngzuò **ne**.

我還沒有工作呢。

(I still haven't found a job yet.)

Pattern 5: With AV: <u>S **hái** pos. / neg. AV FV O **ne**.</u>

Ex: Xiǎo Lǐ **hái** bù néng xiě Zhōngguózì **ne**.

小李還不能寫中國字呢。

(Little Li still cannot write Chinese characters.)

The adverb **hái** in the sense of still may be introduced before the verb to stress continuity. But, its omission will not bring much change in meaning. However, in the negative case, **bù** or **méi** is usually preceded by **hái** to form **hái bù**-V (still not, not yet) or **hái méi**-V (still haven't yet). Furthermore, when **bù**- is followed by a stative or auxiliary verb, equative verb, or even the functive verb, then **méiyǒu** indicates temporary non-attainment of a condition or state.

Ex 1: Háizi **hái bú è ne**.

孩子還不餓呢。

(The children are not yet hungry.)

Ex 2: Nèiběn shū **hái búshì** wǒde **ne**.

那本書還不是我的呢。

(That book isn't mine yet.)

Ex 3: Tā **hái búhuì** huà huàr **ne.**

她還不會畫畫兒呢。

(She still hasn't learned to paint.)

Ex 4: Tā **hái méiyǒu** àirén **ne.**

他還没有愛人呢。

(He still has no wife.)

But, when **bù-** or **méi** is followed by a functive verb, then the speaker is not expressing any immediate change.

Ex 1: Tāmen **hái méi** chàng gēr **ne.**

他們還没唱歌兒呢。

(They haven't sung yet.)

Ex 2: Tā **hái bùdǒng** wǒde xiǎngfa **ne.**

她還不懂我的想法呢。

(She still doesn't understand my viewpoint yet.)

7.3. The Usages of the Modal Particle **Ne**:

A. To make abbreviated questions: From the first two lessons, we learned that **ne** 呢 can present a question in a short form:

Ex 1: Wǒ hěn kě, nǐ **ne**?

我很渴,你呢?

(I am very thirsty, are you?)

Ex 2: Tā shuō dōngxi tài guì, nǐ shuō **ne**?

她說東西太貴,你說呢?

(She says that things are too expensive, what do you say?)

B. To indicate continuous or suspended action (see pattern 7.2. in this lesson).

C. To express uncertainty or for a rhetorical question: To show uncertainty, suspicion, or sarcasm, **ne** is placed at the end of an interrogative sentence which uses such question words as wèishénme 爲什麽 (why), shéi 誰 (who), etc.

Ex 1: Wèishénme wǒ děi gōngzuò **ne**?

爲什麽我得工作呢?

(Why should I work?)

Ex 2: **Shéi** huì ài nǐ **ne**?

誰會愛你呢?

(I wonder who will love you?)

7.4. The Usages of the Modal Particle **Ba** 吧:

117

A.   To make a mild imperative sentence: When **ba** 吧 is placed at the end of an imperative mood sentence, the voice of this imperative sentence becomes milder. **Ba** has the same function as **qǐng** 請, except with a casual manner.

Ex 1: Gěi wǒ shū **ba**.

給我書吧。

(Let me have your book, OK?)

Ex 2: Chī diǎnxin **ba**.

吃點心吧。

(How about having a snack?)

Ex 3: Gěi nǐ **ba**.

給你吧。

(Here, you may have it.)

Ex 4: Bié gàosū nǐ fùmǔ **ba**.

別告訴你父母吧。

(It would be better not to tell your parents.)

B.   To make a mild interrogative sentence: By affixing **ba** to the end of a declarative sentence, questioning on the part of the speaker is implied.

Ex: Nǐmen xiànzài búbì zuò shì **ba**?

你們現在不必做事吧?

(I suppose you don't have to work now.)

Or, the speaker presumes the hearer will probably agree with what he says.

Ex: Nínde háizi dōu bùxiǎo le **ba**?

您的孩子都不小了吧?

(I guess your children are all grown up. Isn't that right?)

C.   To use **hǎo ba** 好吧 while dropping the voice to express unwillingness: With this kind of intonation, the speaker sows reluctance or hesitation in accepting a proposal, challenge or offer.

Ex: "Nín qǐng wǒ chī fàn ba?" "Hǎo ba."

"您請我吃飯吧?" "好吧!"

("How about taking me to dinner?" "Well--, OK.")

PART V.   GRAMMAR NOTES AND OTHERS

1. **Time-Words (TW)**: Time words may be divided into two groups by functions. The first group is "time-when" expressions, which can be used as movable adverbs (and sometimes as nouns) and may stand before or after sentence subjects to indicate the time when the action occurs. They are the key method for showing "tense" (as in English terms). The second group of time words are "time duration" expressions, which are employed to indicate the length of time over which an act did or didn't occur.

2. **The Usage of Zài 再**: The adverb **zài** shows the frequency of action as well as explains the timing of action. **Zài** usually indicates that the action will be repeated or happen again in the future. In addition, **zài** is used by the speaker to suggest that a particular action should take place in the future, for example, **Wǒmen yǐhòu zài shuō ba.** 我們以後再說吧。(Let's talk about it later, okay?)

3. **Zhǐ 只 and Jiù 就**: The adverbs **zhǐ** and **jiù** both may be interpreted as "only," "just," e. g.: **Wǒ zhǐ xǐhuan tā** 我只喜歡他 or **Wǒ jiù xǐhuan tā** 我就喜歡他 (I only like him.) and **Tā zhǐ gěi wǒ yí kuài qián** 他只給我一塊錢 or **Tā jiù gěi wǒ yí kuài qián** 他就給我一塊錢 (He has only given me a dollar.). In this case, **zhǐ** and **jiù** are interchangeable. However, **jiù** has other usages. It is used to introduce subsequent or consequent action and may be translated by "then" or "thereupon." But, these counterparts are more often omitted than expressed in English, while **jiù** is essential in Chinese, e. g., **Tā lǎole, jiù bùxiǎng gōngzuò le.** 他老了，就不想工作了。(When he gets old, then he plans to stop working.) **Jiù** may be interpreted as "soon", and may combine with another auxiliary verb to form such expressions as **jiùyào** 就要 (going to, soon), **jiù děi** 就得 (soon must...) to make a sentence of imminent action, for example, **Wǒmen jiù yào chī fàn le.** 我們就要吃飯了。(We are going to have dinner soon.)

4. **Interrogative Sentences Involving the Modal Particles le 了 and Ne 呢**: In order to make a simple question from the statements having **le** or **ne** as a sentence ending, you may place the interrogative particle **ma** 嗎 right after the modal particle.

   Ex 1: Tā hái hěn yǒuqián **ne ma**?

   他還很有錢呢嗎？

   (Is he still very rich?)

   Ex 2: Nǐ bù xǐhuan wǒ **le ma**?

   你不喜歡我了嗎？

   (Don't you like me any more?)

119

PART VI.   TRANSLATION OF THE TEXT

A Short Story

One day, Gao Gui said to Xiao Qian, "Xiao Qian, you must like hearing stories. In the past, my Chinese was not good enough to understand the stories told by others. But now my Chinese is a little better. Just now, I became acquainted with someone, and he told me a story. Now, I'll repeat the story to you, see if you think it is interesting."

Once upon a time, there was a merchant whose surname was Wen. The Wens owned a small shop which sold coffee and pastries. He had many customers, and business was great.

Mr. and Mrs. Wen had no daughters only a son called Danan. Danan was very lazy. Neither was he willing to study nor did he like to work. He did nothing but play all day long. He often thought:"My father's shop is big and the business is running very well. My family has much money, and with no brothers and sisters, it will all be mine some day. Why should I study or work? Father always tells me to learn the business, this makes me sick. I don't have to listen to him. I'll just go on drinking, dining, and dancing. Now my parents are not so old that they can't work, and when they become old, then I'll think about finding someone to take care of things for me."

One day his mother said to him:"Your father is not feeling well. He can't continue to work any longer. You must learn to do work, because there are not enough of us and the business is very busy." His mother told him that he had to learn to speak tactfully and politely. If he was asked whether the coffee and pastry taste good, he must say:"Yes, I eat them everyday."

So Danan began working. One day, there came a young lady to the shop. She said:"I'm very hungry and thirsty. I would like to have some coffee and cake." Danan answered: "OK. Please be seated." The young lady said:"I often bought your pastries in the past. They were really good. Do you still sell them?"

120

Danan answered:"Yes, we do. Look, how delicious this piece of cake is!" The young lady asked him:"Why do you say this piece is delicious?" Danan answered:"I've tasted it, so I know. I haven't tasted the others, because I am full now."

Lesson 8

The Modification of Nouns

PART I.   TEXT

Dialogue : **Wǔ Huì**--A Dance Party

I.   *Pinyin* Romanization :

Gāo Guì :   Nǐhǎo, Xiǎo Qián. Hǎojǐ tiān bújiàn le, nǐ
                   hǎo ma?

Xiǎo Qián :   Hěnnán shuō, zhèliangtiān wǒ hěnmáng, shàngwǔ,
                   xiàwǔ dōu yǒu kè, lǎoshī tiāntiān dōu gěi wǒmen
                   hěnduō gōngkè, wǒ méiyǒu yìdiǎnr gōngfu. Wǒ
                   xiǎng nèixiē lǎoshī dōu wàngle, xuésheng bù néng
                   zhǐ xuéxí bù wánr a ! Nǐ hǎo ma?

Gāo Guì :   Wǒ yě hěn máng. Yǔfǎkè de lǎoshī cháng
                   jiào wǒmen xiě hěnduō de jùzi, kǒuyǔkè hái hǎo,
                   búdà nán, yě hěn yǒu yìsi. Wǒ jīntiān zhǎo nǐ
                   yǒu yìdiǎnr shì.

Xiǎo Qián :   Zhǎo wǒ yǒu shì? Bú shì yào wǒ gěi nǐ
                   jièshao ge nǚ péngyou ba ! Wǒ xiànzài kě zhēn
                   méiyǒu gōngfu.

Gāo Guì :   Bié kāi wánxiào le ! Shuō zhēnde, bú shì wǒ
                   zhǎo nǐ, shì yí wèi Fǎguó tóngxué yào zhǎo nǐ.

Xiǎo Qián :   Něige Fǎguó tóngxué? Wǒ rènshi ma?

Gāo Guì :   Jiùshì xīnláide nèige, cháng dài ge xiǎo màozi,
                   ài chuān Zhōngguó yīfu, Zhōngguó xié de .

Xiǎo Qián :   Nǐ shuō de búshì Xiǎo Xiè ma? Tā zhǎo wǒ,

122

yǒu shénme shì?

Gāo Guì: Míngtiān wǎnshang wàiguó xuésheng sùshè yǒu
wǔhuì, háiyǒu yīnyuè, jiǔ, diǎnxin..., dàjiā
xiǎng wánrwánr, yě xiǎng qǐng jǐ wèi Zhōngguó
tóngxué cānjiā, suǒyǐ Xiǎo Xiè jiào wǒ zhǎo nǐ.

Xiǎo Qián: Kěshì wǒ bú huì tiàowǔ a!

Gāo Guì: Wǒmen sùshè nánshēng duō, nǚshēng shǎo. Nǐ
búshì rènshi hěn duō nǚtóngxué ma? Qǐng nǐ gěi
wǒmen jièshao jǐ wèi, wǒmen xiǎng qǐng yìxiē
nǚháizi tiào wǔ.

Xiǎo Qián: Nǚtóngxué wǒ rènshi bùshǎo, kěshì wǒ yě bù
zhīdao tāmen něige huì tiàowǔ a!

Gāo Guì: Zhè méi shénme, bú huì tiàowǔde, wǒ kěyǐ jiāo
tā. Zhè bú shì hěn róngyì ma?

Xiǎo Qián: Kěshì, wǒ xuéle hái bú huì tiào ne! Shì bushì
wǒ tài bèn le!

Gāo Guì: Bú shì, nǐ hěn cōngming. Zhōngguó búshì yǒu
jù huà shuō:"Nándе bú huì, hùide bù nán. "Wǒ xiǎng
nǐ bú huì tiào shì jiāo nǐde lǎoshī bú huì jiāo.

II. Chinese Character Version--Regular Form:

舞　會

高貴： 你好,小錢。好幾天不見,你好嗎?

小錢： 很難説,這兩天我很忙,上午,下午都有課,老師天天都給
我們很多功課,我沒有一點兒工夫。我想那些老師都忘
了,學生不能只學習不玩兒啊!你好嗎?

高貴： 我也很忙。語法課的老師常叫我們寫很多的句子,口語課
還好,不大難,也很有意思。我今天找你有一點兒事。

小錢： 找我有事?不是要我給你介紹個女朋友吧!我現在可真

没有工夫。

高貴： 別開玩笑了！說真的，不是我找你，是一位法國同學要找你。

小錢： 哪個法國同學？我認識嗎？

高貴： 就是新來的那個，常戴個小帽子，愛穿中國衣服，中國鞋的。

小錢： 你說的不是小謝嗎？他找我？有什麼事？

高貴： 明天晚上外國學生宿舍有舞會，還有音樂、酒、點心…，大家想玩兒玩兒，也想請幾位中國同學參加，所以小謝叫我找你。

小錢： 可是我不會跳舞啊。

高貴： 我們宿舍男生多，女生少，你不是認識很多女同學嗎？請你給我們介紹幾位，我們想請一些女孩子跳舞。

小錢： 女同學我認識不少，可是我也不知道她們哪個會跳舞啊。

高貴： 這沒什麼，不會跳舞的，我可以教她，這不是很容易嗎？

小錢： 可是，我學了還不會跳呢！是不是我太笨了！

高貴： 不是，你很聰明。中國不是有句話說："難的不會，會的不難。"我想你不會跳是教你的老師不會教。

III. **Chinese Character Version--Simplified Form:**

舞　会

高贵： 你好，小钱。好几天不见，你好吗？

小钱： 很难说，这两天我很忙，上午，下午都有课，老师天天都给我们很多功课，我没有一点儿工夫。我想那些老师都忘了，学生不能只学习不玩儿啊！你好吗？

高贵： 我也很忙。语法课的老师常叫我们写很多的句子，口语课还好，不大难，也很有意思。我今天找你有一点儿事。

小钱： 找我有事？不是要我给你介绍个女朋友吧！我现在可真没有工夫。

高贵： 别开玩笑了！说真的，不是我找你，是一位法国同学要找你。

小钱： 哪个法国同学？我认识吗？

高贵： 就是新来的那个，常戴个小帽子，爱穿中国衣服，中国鞋的。

小钱： 你说的不是小谢吗？他找我？有什么事？

高贵： 明天晚上外国学生宿舍有舞会，还有音乐、酒、点心…，大家想玩儿玩儿，也想请几位中国同学参加，所以小谢叫我找你。

小钱： 可是我不会跳舞啊。

高贵： 我们宿舍男生多，女生少，你不是认识很多女同学吗？请你给我们介绍几位，我们想请一些女孩子跳舞。

小钱： 女同学我认识不少，可是我也不知道她们哪个会跳舞啊。

高贵： 这没什么，不会跳舞的，我可以教她，这不是很容易吗？

小钱： 可是，我学了还不会跳呢！是不是我太笨了！

高贵： 不是，你很聪明。中国不是有句话说："难的不会，会的不难。"我想你不会跳是教你的老师不会教。

PART II.   VOCABULARY--SHĒNGCÍ 生詞

TIME-WHEN EXPRESSIONS (N/MA):

昨天	zuótiān	yesterday
今天	jīntiān	today
明天	míngtiān	tomorrow
上午	shàngwǔ	morning, before noon
中午	zhōngwǔ	noon
下午	xiàwǔ	afternoon

白天		báitiān	daytime
晚上		wǎnshang	evening, night time

Míngtiān wǎnshang nǐ yào
shàng kè ma?

明天晚上你要上課嗎？

(Are you going to attend class
tomorrow evening.)

這兩天	这两天	zhèi liǎng tiān	these couple of days (see note)

Zhèi liǎng tiān nǐde gōngkè máng
bùmáng?

這兩天你的功課忙不忙？

(Have you had a lot of schoolwork
to do in these couple of days?)

那幾天	那几天	nèijǐtiān	those few days

MEASURES (M):

句		jù	(for **huà**-sentence)

Zhèi jù huà wǒ hái bùdǒng.

這句話我還不懂。

(I still don't understand this
sentence.)

件		jiàn	(for clothing, things, etc.)

Nín zuótiān zuòde nèijiàn
shì zhēn bùróngyì.

您昨天做的那件事真不容易。

(The matter that you dealt with
yesterday was very difficult.)

Wǒ chuānde zhèjiàn shì jiù yīfu.

我穿的這件是舊衣服。

(The clothes I am wearing are old.)

NOUNS (N):

句子		jùzi	sentence (M: gè 個)

			Měitiān dōu bié wàngle zuò shí ge jùzi.
			每天都別忘了作十個句子。
			(Please don't forget that you have to write ten sentences every day.)
功課	功课	gōngkè	homework, assignment; course (M: **mén** 門)
			Nǐmende gōngkè máng bumáng?
			你們的功課忙不忙？
			(Do you have a lot of homework?)
工夫		gōngfu	time
			Míngtiān yǒu gōngfu zài zuò ba.
			明天有工夫再做吧。
			(Let's do it again tomorrow, if we have time.)
語法	语法	yǔfǎ	grammar
口語	口语	kǒuyǔ	spoken language
帽子		màozi	hat, cap (M: **gè** 個, **dǐng** 頂)
衣服		yīfu	clothes (M: **jiàn** 件)
大衣		dàyī	overcoat (M: **jiàn** 件)
毛衣		máoyī	sweater (M: **jiàn** 件)
			"Yīfu shì xīnde hǎo, péngyou shì jiùde hǎo." Zhèshì yí jù Zhōngguóde lǎo huà.
			"衣服是新的好，朋友是舊的好。" 這是一句中國的老話。
			"Clothes are best when they're new, friends are best when they're old." This is an old Chinese saying.)
鞋子		xiézi	shoe (M: **zhī** 支), shoes (M: **shuāng** 雙)
一會	一会	-huì	meeting, conference, party
舞會	舞会	wǔhuì	dance party, mixer (lit., dance gathering)
茶會	茶会	cháhuì	tea party

酒會	酒会	jiǔhuì	cocktail party
歡迎會	欢迎会	huānyínghuì	welcome party
宿舍		sùshè	dormitory (lit., sleep in or stay overnight building; see note)
音樂	音乐	yīnyuè	music
男生		nánshēng	male student (see note)
女生		nǚshēng	female student (see note)
同學	同学	tóngxué	classmate, fellow student

FUNCTIVE VERBS (FV):

教		jiāo	teach
			Wáng lǎoshī jiāo shénme kè?
			王老師教什麼課?
			(What course does Prof. Wang teach?)
穿		chuān	wear (clothes, shoes), put on
			Nín chuānde nèijiàn yīfu zhēn hǎokàn.
			您穿的那件衣服真好看。
			(The clothes you are wearing are very pretty.)
			Chuān xīnxié shūfu háishi chuān jiùxié shūfu?
			穿新鞋舒服還是穿舊鞋舒服?
			(Which is more comfortable, wearing new shoes or wearing old shoes?)
戴		dài	wear (hat, cap, watch, etc.), put on
			Nín dài biǎo le ma?
			您戴錶了嗎?
			(Did you wear a watch?)
參加	参加	cānjiā	join in, participate in
			Míngtiān wǒmen qǐng tā chīfàn, nǐ cānjiā ma?
			明天我們請她吃飯,你參加嗎?

128

			(Tomorrow, we'll invite her to dinner, would you like to join us?)
聽說	听说	tīngshuō	hear (it) said
			Tīngshuō, Měiguó xiànzài zhǎo gōngzuò hěn nán.
			聽說，美國現在找工作很難。
			(I heard that it is very difficult to find a job in the U.S. now.)
聽 N 說	听 N 说	tīng N shuō	hear N says...
			Wǒ tīng Lǎo Zhāng shuō nǐ yǒu duìxiàng le.
			我聽老張說你有對象了。
			(I heard Old Zhang say that you have a marriage partner now.)
見	见	jiàn	see, meet; interview (more formal than "kàn")
			Jīntiān xiàwǔ wǒ děi jiàn Zhāng lǎoshī.
			今天下午我得見張老師。
			(This afternoon, I have an appointment to see Prof. Zhang.)
忘		wàng	forget
忘了		wàngle	have forgotten
			Wǒ wàngle tā xìng shénme le.
			我忘了他姓什麼了。
			(I forget what his family name was.)

STATIVE VERBS (SV):

聰明	聪明	cōngming	be intelligent
			Cōngmingrén dōu kěn niàn shū ma?
			聰明人都肯念書嗎？
			(Are the intelligent ones all willing to study?)
笨		bèn	be stupid, clumsy

			Nèige xiǎngfa zhēn bèn. 那個想法真笨。 (That idea is really stupid.)
容易		róngyì	be easy, simple to do Xué Zhōngwén tài róngyì le. 學中文太容易了。 (It is so easy to study Chinese.)
難	难	nán	be difficult, hard to do Xiànzài zuò mǎimai zhēn nán. 現在作買賣真難。 (It is really difficult to do business now.)
難＋FV	难＋FV	nán＋FV	be difficult to do (as the antonym of "hǎo＋FV")
難看	难看	nánkàn	be ugly
難學	难学	nánxué	be difficult to study
難教	难教	nánjiāo	be difficult to teach

VERB-OBJECTS (VO):

請客	请客	qǐng kè	invite guests; entertainment Wǒ xiǎng chī Zhōngguófàn, shéi qǐngkè? 我想吃中國飯，誰請客？ (I want to eat Chinese food, who is going to invite me?)
開玩笑	开玩笑	kāi wánxiào	crack a joke, make fun of Zhè kě búshì kāi wánxiào de shìqing. 這可不是開玩笑的事情。 (This is no joke.)
開會	开会	kāihuì	hold a meeting
有工夫		yǒu gōngfu	have leisure time Wǒmende xuésheng yǒu gōngfu wánr méiyǒu?

我們的學生有工夫玩兒沒有?
(Do our students have time for leisure play?)

Gōngkè tài máng le, méi (yǒu) gōngfu kàn péngyou.

功課太忙了,没(有)工夫看朋友。
(I have too much homework I hardly have any time to visit friends.)

| 教書 | 教书 | jiāo shū | teach school |
| 上課 | 上课 | shàng kè | attend class; class in session |

Shàng kè ne, bié zài wánr le.

上課呢,别再玩兒了。
(Class is in session now. Stop playing.)

Nǐ jīntiān shàng shénme kè ne?

你今天上什麽課呢?
(What course are you taking today?)

| 下課 | 下课 | xià kè | class dismissed, class is over |

Xiànzài xià kè le, wǒmen kěyǐ chàng gēr le.

現在下課了,我們可以唱歌了。
(The class is over, we can sing songs now.)

EXPRESSIONS (EX):

難的不會會的不難		nánde búhuì	What is difficult cannot
难的不会会的不难		huìde bùnán	be done; what can be done is not difficult.
说真的	说真的	shuō zhēnde	be serious
别忘了		bié wàngle	don't forget

PART III. A LIST OF CHARACTERS REQUIRED

TO BE REPRODUCED FROM MEMORY

昨 今 明 上 下 午 晚 句 件 功 課 帽 衣 鞋 宿 舍
音 樂 難 聽 笨 教 容 易 參 加 跳 口 開 忘 見

PART IV.   SENTENCE PATTERNS

8.1.   As a rule, the modifiers always precede the modified expressions. The modification of nouns generally can be divided into two major categories.

A.   The modifiers are single expressions:

1.   A noun is used to modify another noun to form the structure "N1-N2," where N2 is the center word and is modified by N1, which shows the quality, origin, or usage of the noun, such as in **Zhōngwen shū** 中文書 (Chinese books), and **fànzhuō** 飯桌 (dining table). The structural particle **de** 的 is not used as a marker of subordinate construction.

2.   A noun or pronoun used as a modifier to identify the ownership of the modified noun. The structural particle **de** 的 is required as a marker of possession. The structure is formed as "PN/N1 de N2," e.g., **wǒde qián** 我的錢 (my money), **Lǎo Zhāng de shūzhuō** 老張的書桌 (Old Zhang's desk).

3.   Stative verbs as modifiers: Stative verbs can serve as adjectives to describe nouns. Whether the structural particle **de** 的 is required or not depends on the condition of the stative verb. Monosyllabic stative verbs may modify a noun directly without inserting **de** in between, such as **hǎobiǎo** 好錶 (good watch). For polysyllabic stative verbs or stative verbs modified by another adverb, the particle **de** is usually needed, e.g., **hěn hǎotīng de gùshi** 很好聽的故事 (very interesting story). Although these aspects were mentioned in previous lessons, a list of stative verbs, showing whether they require the particle **de** as a noun modifier, is included in Note 1 of this lesson. The modification of nouns in category A is the subject of discussion in previous lessons, however, this is not the main issue of this lesson.

B.   The adjectival modifiers of the subordinate clauses: There are various clauses that act as modifiers of nominal expressions--the center words of sentences. These

132

subordinate clauses, also known for modification of nouns, stand before the modified nominal expressions. In between the nominal element and the subordinate clause is the structural particle **de**, acting as a connector. The word order of this structure is: " modification **de** noun," and this noun can be a subject or an object in a sentence. There are six kinds of subordinate clauses that are used as adjectival modifiers:

1. The modifier is derived from a noun and a verb:

Pattern 1: S   FV   de   N

    Ex: tā chuān de xié

       他穿的鞋

       (the shoes he wears)

This nominal expression **"tā chuān de xié"** can be either a subject or an object in a sentence. For example:

As subject: Tā chuān de xié hěn hǎokàn.

       他穿的鞋很好看。

       (The shoes he wears are good looking.)

As object: Tā fùqīn gěi tā tā chuān de xié.

       他父親給他他穿的鞋.

       (His father has given him the shoes he wears.)

Naturally, we may extend the pattern by adding such supplementary information as:

Pattern 2: S(A) AV FV de N

    Ex: tā bù jiāo de xuésheng

       她不教的學生

       (the student(s) whom she doesn't teach)

2. The modifier is formed by a noun, an auxiliary verb and a functive verb with optional adverb:

Pattern: S FV de N

    Ex: tā xiǎng zhīdao de shìqing

       他想知道的事情

       (the things that he wants to know)

3. The modifier contains a noun, a coverbial expression and a functive verb with optional adverb and auxiliary verb:

Pattern: S (A) (AV) CV-O FV de N

    Ex 1: wǒ mǔqīn yào gěi wǒ mǎi de máoyī

我母親要給我買的毛衣

(the sweater my mother will buy for me)

Ex 2：wǒ búyuànyi gěi tā jièshao de péngyou

我不願意給他介紹的朋友

(the friend whom I don't wish to introduce to him)

Right now, the only coverb we have studied is **gěi** 給 (for), so the coverbial expressions are restricted to the form of "**gěi-person.**" Since the coverbial expressions play an important role in Chinese language, and many more coverbs will be introduced in later lessons, it is beneficial for you to obtain a solid concept regarding this structure now.

4.   The modifier can be derived from a "Verb-object **de**" construction：

Pattern：   FV O de N

Ex 1：   jiāo shū de lǎoshī

教書的老師

(the teacher who teaches)

Ex 2：   zuò shēngyi de shāngrén

做生意的商人

(the merchant who is doing business)

Ex 3：   kāi wǔhuì de sùshè

開舞會的宿舍

(the dormitory where the dance party is held)

In this pattern, if the functive verb refers to a person's occupation and functions as a noun, as in **màibàode** 賣報的 (newspaper seller), **zuòfànde** 做飯的 (cook), **jiāoshūde** 教書的 (teacher), then the modified noun which refers to the person can be omitted. We should note that this kind of expression is rather casual and shows little respect to the individuals thus referred to. Since these expressions are equivalent to nouns, they may be specified, numbered or otherwise modified：

Ex 1：nèige zuòmǎimai de

那個做買賣的

(that merchant)

Ex 2：nà sān ge tiàowǔ de

那三個跳舞的

(those three dancers)

5.   A modifier can be derived from a complete sentence in the form of：

134

Pattern：S FV O de N

   Ex：wǒ gěi tā de màozi

     我給她的帽子

     (the hat I gave her)

6. The numerical expression followed by **de** may stand as a modifier of a nominal expression to indicate price or quantity：

   a. For price：

Pattern 1：Price/Unit **de** N

     Ex：sān máo jiǔ yì zhī **de** bǐ

       三毛九一枝的筆

       (pens at 39 cents apiece)

Pattern 2：Unit/Price **de** N

     Ex：yìshuāng yìbǎi kuài **de** xié

       一雙一百塊的鞋

       (shoes, a pair for $100.00)

   b. For quantity：

Pattern：NU of Person/Unit of Things **de** N

     Ex：yí ge rén yí kuài **de** táng

       一個人一塊的糖

       (candies one person apiece)

C. The modified noun can be generalized by **dōu** 都：Dōu 都 is a totalizer of the nouns which precede it. So, in the structures of modification of nouns, **dōu** may indicate the generalization of the noun：

   Ex 1：Jiāo Zhōngwén de **dōu** shì Zhōngguórén ma?

       教中文的都是中國人嗎？

       (The Chinese language teachers are all Chinese, aren't they?)

   Ex 2：Wǒ shuō de gùshi tā **dōu** bú ài tīng.

       我説的故事他都不愛聽。

       (He doesn't like to hear any of the stories I tell.)

D. The modified noun can be specified by a "SP—NU—M" expression：

   Ex 1：Tā mǎi de nàxiē zhǐ hěn piányi.

       她買的那些紙很便宜。

       (Those papers she bought are very inexpensive.)

Ex 2: Nèizhāng tā huà de huàr zuì hǎokàn.

那張他畫的畫兒最好看。

(That painting he painted is most beautiful.)

8.2.   The Rhetorical Question: For the purpose of emphasis, the rhetorical question is used with a negative expression to stress the affirmative notion. On the other hand, in the absence of a negative expression it stresses the negative. Using the expression **búshì...ma** 不是…嗎 is one of the six popular ways to make rhetcical questions:

Pattern: **búshì** (comment) ma?

Ex: Nǐ búshì hěn ài tiàowǔ ma?

你不是很愛跳舞嗎?

(You like to dance very much, don't you!)

PART V.   GRAMMAR NOTES AND OTHERS

1.   A List of the Stative Verbs (Included in Lessons 1—8) That Serve as Modification of Nouns:

   a.   Stative verbs that stand alone as modifiers of nouns without **de**:

hǎo 好	máng 忙	lèi 累	guì 貴
gāo 高	dà 大	xīn 新	jiù 舊
lǎo 老	lǎn 懶	xiǎo 小	è 餓
kě 渴	ǎi 矮	zǎo 早	nán 難
bèn 笨	cōngming 聰明		

   b.   When any one of the above listed expressions is modified by another adverb, the particle **de** 的 is required for that expression.

   c.   Those requiring the use of **de** 的:

   (1) Any expressions which follow the structure **hǎo**＋FV, **nán**＋FV, such as **hǎotīng de** 好聽的 (the tuneful one), **nánkàn de** 難看的 (the ugly one), etc.

   (2) **Kèqi** 客氣 (be polite), **hěnduō** 很多 (many), **bùshǎo** 不少 (not few), **hěnduì** 很對 (quite right), **yǒuyìsi** 有意思 (interesting), **méiyìsi** 没意思 (boring).

   (3) Ordinarily, the pariticle **de** can be optional: **piányi** 便宜 (cheap), **yǒuqián** 有錢 (rich), **méiqián** 没錢 (poor, not rich), **shūfu** 舒服 (comfortable) and **róngyì** 容易 (easy).

2. The Expressions **Zhèiliǎngtiān** 這兩天 and **Nèijǐtiān** 那幾天： The English equivalent of **tiān** is "day." But **tiān** is also a measure for itself, e. g., **sāntiān** 三天 is "three days." However, once a specifier (SP) precedes "Nu-**tiān**," to form another structure SP-NU-**tiān**, which follows the same format as SP-NU-M-N, such as **nàsāntiān** 那三天 (those three days), the expressions may be classified as "time-when," since it points out a specific period of time.

3. Compare the Usages of **Xuéxí** 學習, **Xué** 學 and **Niàn** 念： These expressions have the meaning of "study," and funciton as verbs. **Xuéxí** was rather formal in Old China, but now is extremely widely used by people of all walks of life in New China. Hence, someone planning to travel to Taiwan would be wiser to avoid using it. **Xué** means to study a particular subject or course. You can say **xué Zhōngwén** 學中文 (study Chinese language), as well as **xué shuō Zhōngguóhuà** 學説中國話 (study how to speak Chinese).

4. To Reply to an Inquiry That Uses a Sentence with a Negative Case： To reply to an inquiry that uses a sentence with a negative case, such as **Nín búlèi ba**? 您不累吧? or **Nín búlèi ma**? 您不累嗎? (You are not tired, are you?) in English, we should say： "Yes, I am tired." or "No, I am not tired." In Chinese, however, you should respond in the opposite way, as **Shì(Yes)**, **wǒ bú lèi**. or **Bù (no)**, **wǒ hěn lèi**. This is because in Chinese the responses "yes" and "no" are comments on the accuracy posed in the hypothesis question.

5. The Expression "SP-NU-M" Used to Indicate the Specification of Nouns： When the expression "SP-NU-M" is used to indicate the specification of nouns, the expression can be placed either at the beginning of the modification or before the modified noun, as in **zhèi jǐ běn wǒ xīn mǎi de shū** 這幾本我新買的書, or **wǒ xīn mǎi de zhèijǐběn shū** 我新買的這幾本書 (these few books I recently purchased), or even when the clause is quite long, the specific can appear twice in both places.

　　Ex 1： Nà liǎng bǎ tā xīn mǎi de yǐzi hěn hǎo.

　　　　　那兩把他新買的椅子很好。

　　　　　(Those two chairs he bought recently are very good.)

　　Ex 2： Nèiwèi hěn gāode, jiāo wǒ Yīngyǔ de Zhāng lǎoshī hěn bú kèqi.

　　　　　那位很高的,教我英語的張老師很不客氣。

　　　　　(That very tall teacher Zhang who teaches me English is very rude.)

6. The suggested chapters in *Essential Grammar for Modern Chinese* are: Chapter IV——Classification of Sentences, (1) The Mood; Chapter VI——The Modification; and Chapter XI——The Structural Particle **De** 的.

PART VI.   TRANSLATION OF THE TEXT

A Dance Party

Gao Gui: Hello, Xiao Qian. Haven't seen you for a couple of
days. How is everything going?

Xiao Qian: It's hard to say. I'm extremely busy these days. I have
classes both in the morning and in the afternoon. The
teachers give a lot of assignments everyday. I have no
free time at all. I wonder whether the teachers have
forgotten that a student cannot have all study and no play.
How have you been?

Gao Gui: I'm busy too. Our grammar teacher always asks us to write
many sentences. My spoken Chinese class is going okay.
It's very interesting and not difficult. I am looking
for you to ask you for a favor.

Xiao Qian: You're looking for me for a favor? You don't mean
to ask me to find a girlfriend for you, do you? I'm
sorry, right now I really have no time to do any
match-making.

Gao Gui: Quit kidding around. To tell you the truth, it's not
I, but a French student who is looking for you.

Xiao Qian: Which French student? Do I know this person?

Gao Gui: It's the new student. He always wears that little hat,
and likes to wear Chinese clothes and Chinese shoes.

Xiao Qian: You must mean Xiao Xie. Why is he looking for me?

Gao Gui: Tomorrow night there will be a party in our foreign
students' dormitory. We'll have music, wine, and
refreshments. We all want to have some fun and enjoy
ourselves. And we'd like to invite some Chinese
students to come to join us. That's why Xiao Xie

	asked me to find you.
Xiao Qian:	But I can't dance.
Gao Gui:	We have a lot more boys than girls in our dormitory. We heard you are popular among girls. We want you to introduce a few girls to us so we can invite them to the party.
Xiao Qian:	It's true I know many girls, but I don't know who among them can dance.
Gao Gui:	That's no problem. I can teach those who can't dance. It's quite easy.
Xiao Qian:	Nevertheless, I've learned how to dance, but I still can't dance well. Maybe I'm too clumsy.
Gao Gui:	Haven't you heard the old Chinese saying: "It's difficult because one doesn't know how. What one knows how to do is not difficult." I suppose your former dance teacher didn't know how to teach.

Lesson 9

Coverb **Zài** for Location and Existence and Expressions of Elative Time

PART I.   TEXT

Dialogue: **Wǒmen de Xiàoyuán**--Our Campus

I.   *Pinyin* Romanization:

Xiè Jiàoshòu: Xiǎo Gāo! Tīngshuō nǐde nǔpéngyou yàolái
                 Běijīng le, shì zhēnde ma?

Gāo Guì: Shéi? Wǒde nǔpéngyou? Nín shuōde shì Ān Měiyīn ba,
                 tā shì wǒ dàxué tóngxué de mèimei. Míngtiān
                 wǎnshang dào.

Xiè Jiàoshòu: Tā shì Wèisīlǐ Dàxué de xuésheng, wǒ hěn xiǎng
                 rènshi tā, nǐ kěyǐ gěi wǒ jièshao jièshao ma?

Gāo Guì: Méiyǒu wèntí! Tā dàole yǐhòu, wǒ jiù jiào tā hé nín
                 jiànjiàn. Míngtiān shì Xīngqīrì, Xīngqīyī wǒ qǐng
                 nín hé tā yì qǐ chīfàn, nín yǒu gōngfu ma?

Xiè Jiàoshòu: Háishì wǒ lái qǐng kè ba, nǐ zài Zhōngguó shì kèrén,
                 bù néng jiào nǐ qǐng a! Ān Měiyīn shì bushì lái xué
                 Zhōngwén a?

Gāo Guì: Bú shì, tā lái gōngzuò. Tā yào zài yí ge wàiyǔ xuéxiàoli
                 jiāo Yīngyǔ, tā zài dàxué xuéde shì Yīngwén.

Xiè Jiàoshòu: Tā xuéde shì Yīngwén, wǒ xuéde yěshì Yīngwén, nǐ zhīdao
                 wǒ wèishénme xiǎng jiàn tā?

Gao Guì: Wǒ tīngshuō nín zài Měiguó de shíhou yěshì zài Wèisīlǐ
                 Dàxué niàn shū.

141

Xiè Jiàoshòu: Duìle, kěshì, nàshì wǔshí duō nián qián de shì le.
Wǒ hěn xiǎng wènwen tā xuéxiào xiànzài de qíngkuàng.
Wǒmen de xiàoyuán zuì měile.

Gāo Guì: Kě bú shì ma! Wǒ xiǎode shíhou jiù zài nèige xiǎochéngli zhù,
wǒ fùqin, mǔqin xiànzài háizài nàr ne, wǒ jiā de fángzi
jiù zài xiàoyuán wàitou de nèi tiáo dàjiē shàng, wǒ
chángcháng zài xiàoyuánli wánr.

Xiè Jiàoshòu: Wǒ zài nàr niànshū de shíhou, yīnwèi xiǎng jiā, yí ge rén
tiāntiān zài hú biān kànkan shān kànkan shuǐ, zài nàr xiěle
bùshǎo jièshao Měiguó shēnghuó qíngkuang de gùshì.
Nèixie gùshì dōu shì xiě gěi wǒ zài Zhōngguó de dìdi
mèimeimen kàn de.

Gāo Guì: Wǒ zhīdao, nínde nèixiē gùshì zài Zhōngguó, zài Měiguó
dōu hěn yǒumíng. Wǒ zài Měiguó dàxué xuéxí Zhōngwén de
shíhòu, hái niànle bùshǎo ne!

Xiè Jiàoshòu: Xiànzài xuéxiào shì bushì yǒule bùshǎo xīn lóu, xīn jiàoshì,
xīn sùshè? Túshūguǎn yě yǒule bùshǎo xīn shū ba? Wǒ xiǎng
túshūguǎn shì yí ge niàn shū de hǎo dìfang.

Gāo Guì: Shì a, kěshì pángbiān de Xuéshēng Zhōngxīn Xīngqīliù wǎn
shang kě zhēn chǎo, yǒu chànggē de, yǒu tiàowǔ de, hái yǒu
bùshǎo rén bú ài zài shítáng chī fàn jiù zài nàr chī.

Xiè Jiàoshòu: Wǒ xiǎng hěnduō dìfang wǒ dōu bú rènshi le, wǒ zài nàr
de shíhou, xuéxiàoli hái méiyǒu jiàotáng, shūdiàn ne. Wǒ zhēn
xiǎng zàiqu kànkan nèi ge hú, kànkan nèi ge ānjìng de
xiàoyuán.

II. Chinese Character Version--Regular Form:

我們的校園

謝教授： 小高！聽説你的女朋友要來北京了，是真的嗎？

高貴： 誰？我的女朋友？您説的是安美音吧，她是我大學同學的妹妹。明天晚上到。

謝教授： 她是衛斯理大學的學生，我很想認識她，你可以給我介紹介紹嗎？

高貴： 沒有問題！她到了以後，我就叫她和您見見。明天是星期日，星期一我請您和她一起吃飯，您有工夫嗎？

謝教授： 還是我來請客吧，你在中國是客人，不能叫你請啊！安美音是不是來學中文啊？

高貴： 不是！她來工作。她要在一個外語學校裏教英語，她在大學學的是英文。

謝教授： 她學的是英文，我學的也是英文，你知道我為什麼想見她？

高貴： 我聽說您在美國的時候，也是在衛斯理大學念書。

謝教授： 對了，可是，那是五十多年前的事了，我很想問問她學校現在的情況。我們的校園最美了。

高貴： 可不是嗎！我小的時候就在那個小城裏住，我父親、母親現在還在那兒呢，我家的房子就在校園外頭的那條大街上，我常常在校園裏玩兒。

謝教授： 我在那兒念書的時候，因為想家，一個人天天在湖邊看看山，看看水，寫了不少介紹美國生活情況的故事。那些故事都是寫給我在中國的弟弟妹妹們看的。

高貴： 我知道，您的那些故事在中國、在美國都很有名。我在美國大學學習中文的時候，還念了不少呢！

謝教授： 現在學校是不是有了不少新樓、新教室，新宿舍？圖書館也有了不少新書吧？我想圖書館是一個念書的好地方。

高貴： 是啊，可是旁邊的學生中心星期六晚上可真吵，有唱歌的，有跳舞的，還有不少人不愛在食堂吃飯就在那兒吃。

謝教授： 我想很多地方我都不認識了，我在那兒的時候，學校裏還沒有教堂、書店呢。我真想再去看看那個湖，看看那個安靜的校園。

我 们 的 校 园

谢教授： 小高！听说你的女朋友要来北京了，是真的吗？

高贵： 谁？我的女朋友？您说的是安美音吧，她是我大学同学的妹妹。明天晚上到。

谢教授： 她是卫斯理大学的学生，我很想认识她，你可以给我介绍介绍吗？

高贵： 没有问题！她到了以後，我就叫她和您见见。明天是星期日，星期一我请您和她一起吃饭，您有工夫吗？

谢教授： 还是我来请客吧，你在中国是客人，不能叫你请啊！安美音是不是来学中文啊？

高贵： 不是！她来工作。她要在一个外语学校里教英语，她在大学学的是英文。

谢教授： 她学的是英文，我学的也是英文，你知道我为什么想见她？

高贵： 我听说您在美国的时候，也是在卫斯理大学念书。

谢教授： 对了，可是，那是五十多年前的事了，我很想问问她学校现在的情况。我们的校园最美了。

高贵： 可不是吗！我小的时候就在那个小城里住，我父亲、母亲现在还在那儿呢，我家的房子就在校园外头的那条大街上，我常常在校园里玩儿。

谢教授： 我在那儿念书的时候，因为想家，一个人天天在湖边看看山，看看水，写了不少介绍美国生活情况的故事。那些故事都是写给我在中国的弟弟妹妹们看的。

高贵： 我知道，您的那些故事在中国、在美国都很有名。我在

144

美国大学学习中文的时候,还念了不少呢!

谢教授: 现在学校是不是有了不少新楼、新教室,新宿舍? 图书
馆也有了不少新书吧?我想图书馆是一个念书的好地
方。

高贵: 是啊,可是旁边的学生中心星期六晚上可真吵,有唱歌
的,有跳舞的,还有不少人不爱在食堂吃饭就在那儿吃。

谢教授: 我想很多地方我都不认识了,我在那儿的时候,学校里
还没有教堂、书店呢。我真想再去看看那个湖,看看那
个安静的校园。

PART II.   VOCABULARY--SHĒNGCÍ 生詞

TIME-WHEN EXPRESSIONS (TW/N/MA):

年	nián (N/M)	year (itself is a measure)
今年	jīnnián	this year
		Jīngnián shì yī jiǔ bā sān nián.
		今年是一九八三年。
		(This year is 1983.)
明年	míngnián	next year
去年	qùnián	last year (lit. , past year)
		Qùnián Sānyuè nǐ zài Zhōngguó ma?
		去年三月你在中國嗎?
		(Were you in China last March?)
月	yuè (N)	month (M: gè 個)
		Zhège yuè wǒ jiā kèrén zhēn duō.
		這個月我家客人真多。
		(We have many guests in our house this month).
一月	Yīyuè	January
二月	Èryuè	February

145

三月	Sānyuè	March
四月	Sìyuè	April
五月	Wǔyuè	May
六月	Liùyuè	June
七月	Qīyuè	July
八月	Bāyuè	August
九月	Jiǔyuè	September
十月	Shíyuè	October
十一月	Shíyīyuè	November
十二月	Shíèryuè	December
星期	Xīngqī(N)	week（M：gè 個）

Zhège xīngqī tài máng le.

這個星期太忙了。

(This week is terribly busy.)

星期天	Xīngqītiān	Sunday
星期日	Xīngqīrì	Sunday
星期一	Xīngqīyī	Monday
星期二	Xīngqīèr	Tuesday
星期三	Xīngqīsān	Wednesday
星期四	Xīngqīsì	Thursday
星期五	Xīngqīwǔ	Friday
星期六	Xīngqīliù	Saturday
日（日子）	rì (or rìzi)	day, date

Yī jiǔ bā sān nián jiǔ yuè
shíliù rì shì xīngqījǐ?

1983年9月16日是星期幾？

(September 16th of 1983 is which
day of the week?)

TIME-WHEN EXPRESSIONS (TW)： A phrase or a clause is formed to indicate when an action is taking place. This type of time-when expression serves as a subordination in a complex sentence (see pattern).

…以前	…yǐqián	…ago, before…

Sān nián yǐqián, wǒmen hái

búrènshi ne.

三年以前，我們還不認識呢。

(We were not acquainted with each
other three years ago.)

Chī fàn yǐqián, nǐ yào zuò
shénme?

吃飯以前，你要做什麼？

(What should you do before eating?)

| 的時候 | 的时候 | ...de shíhòu | when, during, while, at |

Nǐ dào wǒ jiā de shíhòu, wǒ hái zài wàitou ne.

你到我家的時候，我還在外頭呢。

(I was outside of the house when
you arrived.)

| 以後 | 以后 | ...yǐhòu | after, later |

Liǎng nián yǐhòu, nǐde
Zhōngwén jiù hěn hǎo le.

兩年以後，你的中文就很好了。

(In two years from now, your Chinese
will be excellent.)

Nǐ dǒngle yǐhòu, wǒ jiù
búbì zài shuō le.

你懂了以後，我就不必再説了。

(I'll stop explaining right after
you understand it.)

EASURES (M):

		jiā	(for store, shop, etc.)
	层	céng	layer (for story of building, cake)
	间	jiān	space between (for room)
		suǒ	place (for houses, schools, etc.)
	条	tiáo	strip (for things in a long narrow piece, such as street, road, fish, etc.)
		zuò	seat (for cities, hills, buildings,

bridges, etc.)

NOUNS (N):

大學	大学	dàxué	college, university
教授		jiàoshòu	professor (M：**wèi** 位)
生活		shēnghuó	life; to live (N/FV)
情況		qíngkuàng	situation, condition (M：**gè** 個)
城		chéng	city (M：**gè** 個, **zuò** 座)
街		jiē	street, road (M：**tiáo** 條)
山		shān	hill, mountain (M：**zuò** 座)
湖		hú	lake (M：**gè** 個)
樓	楼	lóu	building (of more than one story) (M：**gè** 個, **zuò** 座)
房子		fángzi	house (M：**suǒ** 所)
屋子		wūzi	room (M：**jiān** 間)
時候	时候	shíhòu	time
校園	校园	xiàoyuán	campus (M：**gè** 個)

NOUNS/PLACE WORDS (N/PW)：   Place words are nouns that are preceded by coverbs that show location, starting point or destination. Not every noun may be used as a place word, but some nouns, such as **xuéxiào** 學校 (school), **jiā** 家 (family) refer to a place as well as an institution. Those nouns may be rated as nouns and also as place words.

學校	学校	xuéxiào	school (M：**suǒ** 所)
教堂		jiàotáng	church, chapel (lit., religious hall; M：**gè** 個, **zuò** 座)
教室		jiàoshì	classroom (M：**jiān** 間)
食堂		shítáng	dining hall, cafeteria (lit., eating hall; M：**gè** 個)
書店	书店	shūdiàn	bookstore (M：**gè** 個, **jiā** 家)
一店(一鋪)	(一铺)	-diàn(-pù)	store, shop (M：**gè** 個, **jiā** 家)
學生中心	学生中心	xuéshēng zhōngxīn	student center (M：**gè** 個)
圖書館	图书馆	túshūguǎn	library (M：**gè** 個, **zuò** 座)

PLACE WORDS (PW):

地方		dìfang	place (M：gè 個)
這兒	这儿	zhèr	here (syn. zhèli 這裏)
那兒	那儿	nàr	there (syn. nàli 那裏)
哪兒	哪儿	nǎr	where (syn. nǎli 哪裏?)

The character 兒 for **zhèr**, **nàr** and **nǎr** cannot be omitted in written forms.

PLACE WORD/ADVERB (PW/A):

一起	yìqǐ	together, in the same place
		Tāmen liǎng ge rén chángcháng zài yìqǐ.
		他們兩個人常常在一起。
		(These two always stay together.)
		Hé wǒ zài yìqǐ gōngzuò de shì Lǎo Zhāng.
		和我在一起工作的是老張。
		(The one who works with me is Old Zhang.)

ADVERB (A):

最	zuì	the most, -est

LOCALIZERS (L)：

Localizers are also nouns. In fact, they are the nouns of locality. It may be in bound form and used as a suffix to another noun, such as **-shàng** 上 (on), **shàngtou** 上頭 (top), **zhuōzi shàngtou** 桌子上頭 (on the table, on the top of a table). When the general area is understood from the context, the localizer can be used alone to point out the exact location, e. g., **Nèige lóu méiyou rén zhù, lǐtou méiyǒu dōngxi.** 那個樓沒有人住，裏頭沒有東西。(Nobody lives in that building, it is empty inside.)

一上		-shàng	on
上(頭)	上(头)	shàng(tou)	top; on the top of; above
下(頭)	下(头)	xià(tou)	bottom, below, at the bottom of
裏(頭)	里(头)	lǐ(tou)	inside, inside of, among

一裏	一里	-lǐ (BF)	in
外(頭)	外(头)	wài(tou)	outside, outside of
前(頭)	前(头)	qián(tou)	in front of, in front
後(頭)	后(头)	hòu(tou)	in back of, in rear
底下		dǐxia	underneath
中間兒	中间儿	zhōngjiānr	in the middle of, center
邊	边	-biānr (BF)	side
旁邊兒	旁边儿	pángbiānr	along side, nearby

Nǐ zài wǒ de pángbiānr.

你在我的旁邊兒。

(You are next to me.)

Xiàoyuán pángbiānr yǒu yí
ge hú.

校園旁邊兒有一個湖。

(There is a lake nearby the campus.)

左邊兒	左边儿	zuǒbiānr	left side
右邊兒	右边儿	yòubiānr	right side
上邊兒	上边儿	shàngbiānr	top; on the top of (syn. **shàngtou**)
下邊兒	下边儿	xiàbiānr	bottom; below (syn. **xiàtou**)
前邊兒	前边儿	qiángbiānr	front; in front of (syn. **qiántou**)
後邊兒	后边儿	hòubiānr	back, rear (syn. **hòutou**)
裏邊兒	里边儿	lǐbiānr	inside of (syn. **lǐtou**)
外邊兒	外边儿	wàibiānr	outside (syn. **wàitou**)
這邊兒	这边儿	zhèibiānr	this side
那邊兒	那边儿	nèibiānr	that side
哪邊兒	哪边儿	nǎbiānr	which side?

CONNECTIVE (CONN): A connective is another type of conjunction. It may link two nominal expressions. It is equivalent to "and" in English.

和		hé	and

Měiguó hé Rìběn dōu yǒu
yǒumíng de dàxué.

美國和日本都有有名的大學。

(Both the United States and Japan
have famous universities.)

FUNCTIVE VERBS (FV):

在   zài   be located at (see pattern and note; it must be followed by PW)

Nínde àirén yě zài Zhōngguó ma?

您的愛人也在中國嗎？

(Is your spouse also in China?)

到   dào   reach, arrive

Tā qùnián shénme shíhou dào nàr de?

他去年什麼時候到那兒的？

(When did he reach there last year?)

住   zhù   reside, stay (for overnight), live

Nín zài shénme dìfang zhù?

您在什麼地方住？

(Where do you live?)

寫給   写给   xiěgěi   write to, write for (it is a compound verb; gěi acts as a post verb with the same function as it has in the expression "màigěi—")

念   niàn   read, read aloud, study (a course or subject)

Niàn Zhōngwén bùnán ba.

念中文不難吧。

(Studying Chinese is not hard, I suppose.)

STATIVE VERBS (SV):

安静   ānjìng   quiet, silent, peaceful

Wǒmen xuéxiào de xuésheng tài ānjìng, búài shuōhuà.

我們學校的學生太安静，不愛説話。

(The students of our school are too

151

			shy, they don't like to speak up.)
吵		chǎo (SV/FV)	be noisy, clamorous; quarrel

Xuéshēng Zhōngxīn zhēn chǎo.
學生中心真吵。
(The Student Center is really clamorous.)

Ānjìng yìdiǎnr, bié zài chǎo le.
安静一點兒，別再吵了。
(Be quiet! Stop quarreling.)

美		měi	be pretty, beautiful

Nèige nǚshēng zhēn měi, rénrén dōu ài kàn tā.
那個女生真美，人人都愛看她。
(That woman student is really pretty, eveybody loves to look at her.)

有名		yǒumíng	be famous, be well-known

Nín zhùde nèige chéng hěn yǒumíng.
您住的那個城很有名。
(The city you reside in is very famous.)

COVERBS (CV):

在		zài	at, in, on, etc. (must precede a PW indicating the location, see pattern and note)

Wǒ zài Zhōngguó xuéxí Zhōngwén ne.
我在中國學習中文呢。
(I am studying Chinese in China now.)

來	来	lái	to; for (intro. purpose of action, see note)

Fàn, wǒ lái chī, shìqing,

tā lái zuò.

飯，我來吃，事情，他來做。

(I eat the food, but he does the work.)

VERB-OBJECT (VO):

念書	念书	niàn shū	study, read

Nǐ zài nǎr niàn shū?

你在哪兒念書？

(Where do you study?)

PROPER NAMES: Names of Some Cities (see note):

北京		Běijīng	Beijing
波士頓	波士顿	Bōshìdùn	Boston
紐約	纽约	Niǔ Yuē	New York City
上海		Shànghǎi	Shanghai
臺北	台北	Táiběi	Taibei
香港		Xiānggǎng	Hong Kong

Names of Some Colleges and Universities:

北京大學	北京大学	Běijīng Dàxué	Beijing University
臺灣大學	台湾大学	Táiwān Dàxué	Taiwan University (in Taibei)
衛斯理大學	卫斯理大学	Wèisīlǐ Dàxué	Wellesley College
麻省理工學院	一学—	Má Shěng Lǐ -Gōng Xuéyuàn	M. I. T.
哈佛大學	一学—	Hā Fó Dàxué	Harvard University

PART III.   A LIST OF CHARACTERS REQUIRED
TO BE REPRODUCED FROM MEMORY

地 方 房 屋 街 圖 館 室 山 湖 樓 時 候 校 頭 裏

153

左右邊旁間底安静吵月星期年同住活
況封念最

PART IV.　　SENTENCE PATTERNS

9.1.　　Place Words and Localizers：　　The main topic in this lesson is the function and usage of the verb **zài** 在, both as a coverb and as a functive verb. A place word is required by **zài** 在 as long as **zài** 在 is a stationary verb that indicates the locality of the subject, or of the action. Thus, it is clear that locality may be denoted by a proper noun, a localizer or a combination of noun plus localizer.

A.　　Proper nouns as place words：Names of countries and cities can be used as place words and do not need localizers, such as **Niǔ Yuē** 紐約 (New York), **Běijīng** 北京 (Beijing), **Táiběi** 臺北 (Taipei), **Zhōngguó** 中國 (China), and **Yìdàlì** 意大利 (Italy), etc. But the names of geographical entities that are not administrative areas, such as rivers, mountains, lakes, etc., cannot form place words without localizers, for example, **Báishān pángbiānr** 白山旁邊兒 (nearby White Mountain), **Wěibīnghú shàng** 慰冰湖上 (on Lake Waban), etc.

B.　　Nouns as place words：Nouns such as **jiàotáng** 教堂 (church), **dàxué** 大學 (college, university), **túshūguǎn** 圖書館 (library) refer to a place as well as an institution. The use of the appropriate localizer is required only when a particular part of the building is mentioned.

　　　　Ex 1：Wǒmen xuéxiào hěn yǒumíng. (without a localizer)

　　　　　　我們學校很有名.

　　　　　　(Our school is very famous.)

　　　　Ex 2：Jīntiān jiàotáng lǐtou méiyǒu rén. (with a localizer)

　　　　　　今天教堂裏頭沒有人.

　　　　　　(There is no one in the church today.)

C.　　Common nouns plus localizers：To show which part of a given noun serves as a place of reference, the construction "Common Noun ＋ Localizer" must be adopted. The structural particle **de** 的 is not required for this pattern.

Pattern："Common Noun＋Localizer"

　　Ex 1：zhuōzi shàngtou (on the table)

　　　　桌子上頭

154

Ex 2: yǐzi dǐxia (underneath the chair)

椅子底下

Ex 3: kāfēili (in the coffee)

咖啡裏

Ex 4: fángzi qiántou (in front of the house)

房子前頭

Ex 5: bàoshang (in the newspaper)

報上

9.2. **The Functive Verb Zài 在:** Zài 在 may serve as a main verb in a sentence to refer to place where the subject of the sentence is found. The appropriate place words are always required.

Pattern: S (A) (AV) zai PW.

Ex: Gāngcái tā búzài jiā, kěshì, xiànzài zàijiā le.

剛才他不在家,可是,現在在家了。

(Just a while ago, he wasn't at home, but now he is home.)

9.3. **Zài 在 Is Used as a Coverb Pertaining to Location:**

Pattern: S (A) (AV) zài-PW FV (Mod.) O.

Ex 1: Wǒmen hěn xǐhuan zài chéngwàitou zhù.

我們很喜歡在城外頭住。

(We enjoy living outside of the city very much.)

Ex 2: Tā bú ài zài túshūguǎn kàn shū.

她不愛在圖書館看書。

(She doesn't like to read in the library.)

Ex 3: Tā búzài túshūguǎn kànshū.

她不在圖書館看書。

(She doesn't read in the library.)

When the sentence is in a negative form, usually it is constructed by negating the verb in a sentence which has either an auxiliary verb or a coverb. The main verb may be negated only if there are two actions that are to be contrasted. The contrast is apparent when the clause with the negated functive verb is followed by a positive clause.

Ex: Tā zài jiǔdiàn méi hē jiǔ, tā zuò shì ne.

她在酒店没喝酒,她做事呢。

(She didn't drink in a liquor store; she worked there.)

9. 4. The Function of Coverbial Phrase **Zài** 在—PW When Positioned at the Beginning of a Sentence: Whenever a coverbial phrase **zài**—PW appears at the very beginning of a sentence, it is used to stress the location or existential status of the subject which can be either animate or inanimate. The presence of the verb **yǒu** 有 immediately after the coverbial phrase **zài**—PW holds the key to distinguishing the locational function from the existential one.

A. When the coverbial phrase **zài**—PW immediately precedes the subject of the sentence it modifies, the nature of the sentence is "topic-comment." The function of the coverbial phrase is to bestow particular attention to the location where the speaker's comment on the topic applies.

Pattern: <u>**Zài**—PW, Topic Comment.</u>

(Zài—PW, S V O).

Ex 1: Zài Xuéshēng Zhōngxīn, tā chàngde gēr zuì hǎoting.

在學生中心,他唱的歌兒最好聽。

The songs he sings are the most beautiful ones heard in the Student Center.)

Ex 2: Zhèr, cōngmingde xuésheng tài duō le.

這兒,聰明的學生太多了。

(Here, intelligent students are numerous.)

Ex 3: **Zài** wǒmen shāngdiàn, tā shì yí ge hěn lǎn de diànyuán.

在我們商店,他是一個很懶的店員。

(In our shop, he is a very lazy clerk.)

B. This coverbial phrase, **zài**+PW, can also be followed by the verb **yǒu**+object. The subject of this sentence is indeterminate. The aim of the speaker is to highlight the existential status of the subject. Everything must exist within a special or conceptual framework, hence, the inclusion of this coverbial phrase at the begining of the sentence, e. g,. **zài zhuōzi shàng** 在桌子上 (on the table).

9. 5. Modification of Nouns Indicated by **Zài** 在-PW: In Lesson 8, we briefly discussed the use of a coverbial expression to modify a noun, as in **gěi tā mǎishū de qián** 給她買書的錢(the money given to her to buy books). Here, we discuss in greater depth how to use a coverbial expression to modify nouns.

A. Use place words as modifiers:

Pattern: <u>(**Zài**) PW de Noun</u>

Ex: (**Zài**) zhuōzishang de shū

(在)桌子上的書

(the book on the table)

Ex：(zài) Zhuōzishang de shū shì wǒ de.

（在）桌子上的書是我的。

(The book on the table is mine.)

Ex：(Zài) Wǒmen zhèr de xuésheng dōu cōngming.

（在）我們這兒的學生都聰明。

(The students at our place are all intelligent.)

Ex：Chéng wàitou de fángzi piányi yìdiǎnr ba.

城外頭的房子便宜一點兒吧。

(The houses in the countryside are a little cheaper, I guess.)

Ex：Qǐng gěi wǒ zài zhōngjiānr de nèiběn huàbào.

請給我在中間兒的那本畫報。

(Please give me that pictorial magazine in the middle.)

Here, only when the coverbial expression is either very long or contains quite a few words, is the coverb **zài** necessary. Otherwise, a coverb is not required. Let us take a more complicated structure as an example：

Pattern：(A) (AV) **Zài**—PW FV (Mod.) O de Noun

Ex：xǐhuan **zài** húbiānrshang kàn shū de xuésheng

喜歡在湖邊兒上看書的學生

(the student who likes to read along the lake shore)

Ex：Nà ge xǐhuan **zài** húbiānrshang kànshū **de** xuésheng shì wǒ nǚer.

那個喜歡在湖邊兒上看書的學生是我女兒。

(That student who likes to read along the lake shore is my daughter.)

Ex：**Zài** Běijīng chéngwàitou gōngzuò **de** rén yǒu duōshǎo?

在北京城外頭工作的人有多少？

(How many people are working outside the city of Beijing?)

B.   Modification of nouns by localizers：Localizers are also place words. Except for those bound-form monosyllabic localizers, such as —**tóu** 頭，—**li** 里，—**biān** 邊，the localizers can modify nouns. The structural particle **de** 的 is required for this structure.

Pattern：L   de   N

Ex：**shàngtou** de shū

上頭的書

(the book on the top)

Ex：Wǒ yào **shàngtou** de nèiběn shū.

我要上頭的那本書。

(I want the book on the top.)

Ex：qiántou de dà lóu

前頭的大樓

(the tall building in front)

Ex：Qiántou de dà lóu shì yì suǒ xuéxiào.

前頭的大樓是一所學校。

(The tall building in front is a school.)

Ex：wàitou de jiàoshì

外頭的教室

(the classroom outside)

Ex：Wàitou de jiàoshì yǒu rén shàng kè ne.

外頭的教室有人上課呢。

(A class is held in the classroom outside.)

9.6.   **Specific Expressions of Relative Time**：   Some words, phrases and nouns can be followed immediately by yǐqián 以前 (before), de shíhou 的時候 (during) or yǐhòu 以
後 (after), etc. This group of time-when expressions are also movable expressions.
The sentences they form are always subordinate sentences.

A.   With expression **Yǐqián** 以前：

1. The expression "NU—M—N—**yǐqián**" show how long ago.

Pattern：<u>NU—M—N—**yǐqián**</u>, clause.

Ex：sì ge yuè yǐqián

四個月以前

(four months ago)

Ex：(Zài) Sì ge yuè yǐqián, wǒ hái búhuì shuō Zhōngguóhuà ne.

（在）四個月以前，我還不會説中國話呢。

(Four months ago, I did not know how to speak Chinese.)

2. With a specific period of time：

Pattern：<u>(Zài) SP—NU—M—N—yǐqián</u>, clause.

Ex：nà liǎng ge xīngqī yǐqián

那兩個星期以前

(those two weeks ago)

Ex：(Zài) Nà liǎng ge xīngqī yǐqián, wǒ rènshìle Lǎo Zhāng.

（在）那兩個星期以前，我認識了老張。

(I became acquainted with Old Zhang before these two weeks.)

3. Before the occurrence of a particular action：

Pattern：<u>(Zài) S V O yǐqián</u>, clause.

Ex：(Zài) wǒ mǎi dōngxi yǐqián

(在)我買東西以前

(before I go shopping)

Ex：(Zài) Wǒ mǎi dōngxi yǐqián, tā gěile wǒ yìdiǎnr qián.

(在) 我買東西以前,他給了我一點兒錢。

(He gave me some money before I go shopping.)

4. Before a certain date：

Pattern：Date—yǐqián, clause.

Ex：(Zài) yī jiǔ qī wǔ nián yǐqián

(在) 一九七五年以前

(before 1975)

Ex：(Zài) Yī jiǔ qī wǔ nián yǐqián, wǒ búzài Měiguó.

(在) 一九七五年以前,我不在美國。

(I wasn't in the States before 1975.)

B.　　With ... de shíhou ···的時候：

Pattern：(Zài) S V O de shíhou, clause.

Ex：(Zài) Tā qǐng kè de shíhou

(在) 他請客的時候

(when he invites guests)

Ex：(Zài) Tā qǐng kè de shíhou, wǒ yàole yí ge zuìguì de cài.

(在)他請客的時候,我要了一個最貴的菜。

(I ordered a most expensive dish when he invited me.)

C.　　With the expression ... yǐhòu... 以後：

1. For after a period of time：

Pattern：(Zài) NU—M—N—yǐhòu, clause

Ex：(Zài) qītiān yǐhòu

(在)七天以後

(after seven days / seven days later)

Ex：(Zài) Qītiān yǐhòu, tā jiù dào zhèr le.

(在) 七天以後,她就到這兒了。

(She will arrive here after seven more days.)

2. After a specific period of time：

Pattern：(Zài) SP—NU—M—N—yǐhòu, clauses.

Ex：(Zài) nà sān nián yǐhòu

（在）那三年以後

(after those three years)

Ex：Nà sānnián yǐhòu, wǒ wàngle cóngqián de shìqing.

那三年以後，我忘了從前的事情。

(I forgot all past affairs after those three years.)

3. After a certain action is completed：The adverb jiù 就 is used in the second clause, which is the main clause in this structure.

Pattern：(Zài) S V (le) O yǐhòu, clause.

Ex：wǒ zuòle gōngkè yǐhòu

我做了功課以後

(after I finish my homework)

Ex：Wǒ zuòle gōngkè yǐhòu, wǒmen jiù kěyǐ wánr le.

我做了功課以後，我們就可以玩兒了。

(We'll be able to play after I finish my homework.)

4. After a certain date：

Pattern：Zài date yǐhòu, clause.

Ex：Zài èr líng líng yī nián yǐhòu

在2001年以後

(after the year of 2001)

Ex：Zài èr líng líng yī nián yǐhòu, něiguó zuì yǒu qián?

在2001年以後，哪國最有錢？

(After the year of 2001, which country will be the richest?)

PART V.   GRAMMAR NOTES AND OTHERS

1.   Chinese Characters with More Than One Pronunciation or Tone：   There are a large number of Chinese characters that assume more than one pronunciation or tone, as they assume different usages or functions. For instance, as a functive verb, the pronunciation of jiāo 教 (to teach) is the first tone. When it is used as a noun, however, as in jiàoshòu 教授 (professor), jiàoshì 教室 (classroom) or jiàotáng 教堂 (church), the pronunciation of jiào 教 is in the fourth tone.

2. As a Coverb, **Zài** 在 has Many Prepositional Equivalents in English： It can variously mean： in, on, at, above, under, behind, in front, underneath, etc. The best way to ascertain the meaning of **zài** 在 is to look at the noun and localizer that follow it, e. g.： **zài wūzi qiántou** 在屋子前頭 (in front of the house), **zài shū xiàtou** 在書下頭 (under the book), and **zài jiàotáng wàitou** 在教堂外頭 (outside the church).

3. The Coverb **Zài** 在 May Take a Time-When Expression： The coverb **zài** 在 not only can have a place word as its object, but also may take a time-when expression, such as **zài tā chàng gēr de shíhou** 在她唱歌兒的時候 (when she is singing), **zài wǒ xuéxí Yīngyǔ yǐqián** 在我學習英語以前 (before I started to learn English), and **zài nǐ dàole Běijīng yǐhòu** 在你到了北京以後 (after you arrive in Beijing). Since these expressions are movable adverbs when any of them is placed before the subject, the word **zài** 在 is optional. On the other hand, if these time-when expressions are preceded by subjects, **zài** is required, e. g. , **Tā zài wǒ xuéxí Yīngyǔ yǐqián, chángcháng hé wǒ yìqǐ shuō Zhōngguohuà.** 他在我學習英語以前，常常和我一起說中國話. (He and I always chatted in Chinese before I started to learn English.)

4. How to Translate the English Verb "to Be" into Chinese： The English verb "to be " is used in several different senses, each of which has a distinct rendering in Chinese, such as：

Descriptive：America **is** beautiful.   Měiguó hěn **měi**. （as SV）
Equative： That **is** a desk.   Nèi **shì** shūzhuō. （as EV）
Locative： She **is** at school.   Tā **zài** xuéxiào. （as FV "**zài**"）
Indeterminative
Subject： There **is** a pen.   Yǒu yì zhī bǐ. （as FV "**yǒu**"）

5. Some Functions of **Shì** 是： In addition to being used as an equative verb, **shì** 是 also carries the following functions：

A.   **Shì** 是 used for emphasis： For example, to say "Is he very busy?" we may use **Tā hěn máng ma?** But if we would like to stress the voice, we can say **Tā shì bushì hěn máng?** 他是不是很忙? or **Tā hěn mǎng, shì bushì?** 他很忙，是不是?

B.   Use of **kě búshì ma?** 可不是嗎? ： **Kě búshì ma?**, used as a rhetorical question, can also be used as a device for emphasis.

6. Dates are Read Differently in Chinese： Basically, the sequence of time names always begins with the bigger unit, followed by progressively smaller ones, for instance, "year, month, week, day, division of day, time by the clock. " So, the evening of December

24, 1983, should be read in Chinese as: **Yī jiǔ bā sān nián shí·èr yuè èrshí sì rì wǎnshang** 1983年12月24日晚上.

7. Uses of **Lái** 來: **Lái** 來 basically is an intransitive verb with the English equivalent of "to come." However, **lái** may also function as a coverb to introduce the purpose of certain actions. Here, in the sentence of **Kè, wǒ lái qǐng** 客，我來請 (Let me invite you.) **lái** presents the action which is **qǐngkè** in a casual but persistent way.

8. Foreign Proper Names: Foreign proper names are usually transliterated to the native pronunciation, but a few contain translation by meaning, such as:

Little Rock City 小石城
New Jersey 新澤西
Salt Lake City 鹽湖城

9. The suggested chapters in *Essential Grammar for Modern Chinese* for this lesson are: Chapter VII——Determinatives and Measures; Chapter VIII——The Equative Verb **Shì** 是 and the Functive Verb **Yǒu** 有; and Chapter XIII——Coverb (2); **Zài** 在 for Location and Existence.

PART VI.   TRANSLATION OF THE TEXT

Our Campus

Prof. Xie: Xiao Gao, I heard that your girlfriend will be arriving in
Beijing tomorrow. Is it true?

Gao Gui: Who? My girlfriend? Oh, you must be talking about An Meiyin. She
is the younger sister of my college classmate. She'll arrive tomorrow
evening.

Prof. Xie: She is a student at Wellesley College. I would like to meet her. Could
you introduce me to her?

Gao Gui: Yes. It's no problem at all. I'll ask her to see you after she arrives.
Tomorrow is Sunday. Next Monday I'll invite both of you for dinner.
Do you have time?

Prof. Xie: Let me invite you folks. You are a guest in China. I cannot let
you be the host. Is An Meiyin here to study Chinese?

Gao Gui: No, she is not. She is coming to work. She'll be teaching English
at a foreign language school. She majored in English when she was
a college student.

Prof. Xie: She majored in English. That was also my major. Do you know why
I'm so anxious to meet her?

Gao Gui: I heard that you also studied at Wellesley when you were in the
States.

Prof. Xie: Right! But that was more than fifty years ago. I am anxious
to find out the latest about my Alma Mater from her. Our campus is
the most beautiful. . . .

Gao Gui: Isn't that so! I spent my childhood in that town, and my parents
are still there. Our house is on that main street right off the
campus. I spent a lot of time on the campus.

Prof. Xie: While I was studying there, I was often very homesick, so I spent
a lot of time by the lake shore, enjoying the scenery. There I also
wrote quite a few stories about life in the States. Those stories

	were for my little brothers and sisters in China.
Gao Gui:	Oh! Now I know. Those stories of yours are very well-known both in China and the States. I studied a good number of them in my Chinese class at school in the States.
Prof. Xie:	There must be many new buildings, classrooms, and dormitories on campus now. I'll bet there are also many new books in the library. I imagine that the library is an ideal place for studying.
Gao Gui:	It's true. However, the student center which is next to the library is really noisy on Saturday night. There are people singing and dancing, and even people eating there because they cannot stand the dorm food.
Prof Xie:	I guess there must be many places I wouldn't recognize. The buildings, such as the chapel, and the bookstore weren't there during my time. I really want to go back and see that lake, that peaceful and beautiful campus again.

Lesson 10

Coverbs Pertaining to Movement

PART I.   TEXT

Yìfēng Jiāxìn--A Letter Home

I.   *Pinyin* Romanization:

Shíyīyuè de yí ge Xīngqīliù, Gāo Guì chīle wǔfàn, bù xiǎng dào jiēshang qù, yě bù xiǎng qù túshūguǎn wēnxí gōngkè. Tóngxuémen dōu qù wánr le, jiù tā yí ge rén zài wūzili, tā bù zhīdao yīnggāi zuò shénme, suànsuan Gǎn'ēn jié kuài dào le, jīnnián tā bù néng huíjiā guòjié, tā fēicháng xiǎng jiā, xiǎng chī mǔqīn zuòde huǒjī! Tā xiǎng, tā yídìng děi xiě fēng xìn, gàosu fùmǔ tā zài Zhōngguó shàngxué de qíngkuàng.

Gāo Guì de jiāxìn shì zhème xiě de:
Qīn'ài de bàba, māma:

Nǐmen hǎo! Māma Shíyuè èrshíbā rì xiěgěi wǒ de xìn, jīntiān shōu dào le. Zài guówài kàn jiāxìn zhēn shì yí jiàn zuì kuàilè de shì! Xiànzài, wǒ kěshi zhīdao "jiāshū dǐ wànjīn" de yìsi le.

Shàng ge yuè wǒ hé tóngxuémen qí zìxíngchē dào xiāngshān qù wánr, kànjiànle shānshang de hóngyè. Wǒ xiǎng Wèisīlǐ xiànzài yídìng yěshì zuì hǎokàn de shíhou. Wǒ duōme xiǎng zuò fēijī huíjiā kànkan, hé bàba, māma yìqǐ guò Gǎn'ēn jié a! Kěshì, kuài kǎoshì le, yīnwèi yào wēnxí gōngkè, wǒ hái děi zài xuéxiàoli.

Wǒ de xuéxí hé shēnghuó qíngkuàng dōu hěn búcuò. Yīnwèi máng, suǒyǐ fēicháng lèi. Měitiān zǎoshang zǎofàn yǐqián, wǒ dōu duànliàn shēntǐ. Shàngwǔ qí chē qù shàngkè. Wǔfàn zài xuéxiào de shítáng chī, fàn hěn búcuò. Xiàwǔ xiàle kè, wǒ jiù dào jiēshang zǒuzou. Wǎngfàn yǐhòu, wǒ cháng zài sùshèli zhǔnbèi gōngkè, yě chángcháng dào xuéxiào pángbiān de diànyǐngyuàn kàn diànyǐng, yǒu de shíhou yě kànkan diànshì. Wǒ bù xǐhuan qù túshūguǎn, nàr de rén tài duō, bù yídìng yǒu dìfang zuò. Wǒ xiànzài cháng hé Zhōngguó péngyoumen yìqǐ shuōhuà, hái néng shuō Zhōngwén gùshi ne.

Xīnnián de shíhou, wǒ hé jǐ ge tóngxué zhǔnbèi cóng Běijīng zuò huǒchē dào Shànghǎi qù kànkan, zài cóng Shànghǎi zuò chuán dào Xiānggǎng qù wánr yí ge xīngqī, huí Běijīng yǐhòu zài gěi nǐmen xiě xìn.

Zhù

Jiànkāng, kuàilè!

Nǐmen de érzi
Gāo Guì
1983. 11. 5

II.   Chinese Character Version--Regular Form：

一 封 家 信

　　十一月的一個星期六，高貴吃了午飯，不想到街上去，也不想去圖書館溫習功課。同學們都去玩兒了，就他一個人在宿舍裏。他不知道應該做什麼，算算感恩節快到了，今年他不能回家過節，他非常想家，想吃母親做的火雞！他想，他一定得寫封信。告訴父母他在中國上學的情況。

　　高貴的家信是這麼寫的：
親愛的爸爸、媽媽：

　　你們好！媽媽十月二十八日寫給我的信，今天收到了。在國外看家信真是一件最快樂的事！現在，我可是知道"家書抵萬金"的意思了。

　　上個月我和同學們騎自行車到香山去玩兒，看見了山上的紅葉。我想衛斯理現在一定也是最好看的時候。我多麼想坐飛機回家看看,和爸爸、媽媽一起過感恩節啊! 可是,快考試了,因爲要溫習功課,我還得在學校裏。

　　我的學習和生活情況都很不錯。因爲忙。所以非常累。每天早上早飯以前,我都鍛煉身體。上午騎車去上課。午飯在學校的食堂吃,飯很不錯。下午下了課,我就到街上走走。晚飯以後我常在宿舍裏準備功課,也常常到學校旁邊的電影院看電影,有的時候也看看電視。我不喜歡去圖書館,那兒的人太多,不一定有地方坐。我現在常和中國朋友們一起說話,還能説中文故事呢。

　　新年的時候,我和幾個同學準備從北京坐火車到上海去看看,再從上海坐船到香港去玩兒一個星期,回北京以後再給你們寫信。

　　　　祝

　　健康,快樂!

　　　　　　　　　　　　你們的兒子
　　　　　　　　　　　　　　高貴
　　　　　　　　　　　　1983. 11. 5

III. Chinese Character Version--Simplified Form：

一 封 家 信

　　十一月的一个星期六,高贵吃了午饭,不想到街上去,也不想去图书馆温习功课。同学们都去玩儿了,就他一个人在宿舍里。他不知道应该做什么,算算感恩节快到了,今年他不能回家过节,他非常想家,想吃母亲做的火鸡! 他想,他一定得写封信。告诉父母他在中国上学的情况。

高贵的家信是这么写的：

亲爱的爸爸、妈妈：

你们好！妈妈十月二十八日写给我的信，今天收到了。在国外看家信真是一件最快乐的事！现在，我可是知道"家书抵万金"的意思了。

上个月我和同学们骑自行车到香山去玩儿，看见了山上的红叶。我想卫斯理现在一定也是最好看的时候。我多么想坐飞机回家看看，和爸爸、妈妈一起过感恩节啊！可是，快考试了，因为要温习功课，我还得在学校里。

我的学习和生活情况都很不错。因为忙，所以非常累。每天早上早饭以前，我都锻炼身体。上午骑车去上课。午饭在学校的食堂吃，饭很不错。下午下了课，我就到街上走走。晚饭以後我常在宿舍里准备功课，也常常到学校旁边的电影院看电影，有的时候也看看电视。我不喜欢去图书馆，那儿的人太多，不一定有地方坐。我现在常和中国朋友们一起说话，还能说中文故事呢。

新年的时候，我和几个同学准备从北京坐火车到上海去看看，再从上海坐船到香港去玩儿一个星期，回北京以後再给你们写信。

祝

健康，快乐！

你们的儿子
高贵
1983. 11. 5

PART II.　　VOCABULARY--SHĒNGCÍ 生詞

TIME-WHEN EXPRESSIONS (TW/N/MA):

上月		shàngyuè	last month
這(個)月	这(个)	zhè(ge)yuè	this month
下(個)月	下(个)	xià(ge) yuè	next month
上星期		shàngxīngqī	last week
這星期	这星期	zhèixīngqī	this week
下星期		xiàxīngqī	next week
早上		zǎoshàng	morning, early morning
有(的)時候	一时候	yǒu(de)shíhou	sometimes, at times

Wǒ bùcháng cānjiā wǔhuì,
yǒu (de) shíhou qù.

我不常參加舞會，有(的)時候去。

(I don't go to dance parties
very often, just every now and then.)

Sùshèli yǒushíhòu yě hěn ānjìng.

宿舍裏有時候也很安静。

(Sometimes it is also very quiet
in the dormitory.)

MEASURES (M):

輛	辆	liàng	(for vehicles)
封		fēng	(for letters)
架		jià	(for airplanes, television sets)

NOUNS (N):

早飯	早饭	zǎofàn	breakfast (M：dùn 頓)
午飯	午饭	wǔfàn	lunch (M：dùn 頓)
中飯	中饭	zhōngfàn	lunch (M：dùn 頓)
晚飯	晚饭	wǎnfàn	dinner (M：dùn 頓)
火鷄	火鸡	huǒjī	turkey (lit., fire-chicken;

169

			M：**zhǐ** 只）
信		xìn	letter (M：**fēng** 封）
家信		jiāxìn	letter to home；letter from home
信紙	信纸	xìnzhǐ	stationery (M：**zhāng** 張）
信封		xìnfēng	envelope (M：**gè** 個）
自行車	自行车	zìxíngchē	bicycle (lit.，self-propelled vehicle；M：**liàng** 輛）
汽車	汽车	qìchē	car，vehicle (M：**liàng** 輛）
校車	校车	xiàochē	school bus (M：**liàng** 輛）
公(共)(汽)車	一车	gōng(gòng) (qì) chē	bus (lit.，public vehicle；M：**liàng** 輛）
地鐵	地铁	dìtiě	subway (lit.，underground railway；M：**jié** 節 for a car）
火車	火车	huǒchē	(railroad) train (M：**jié** 節）
飛機	飞机	fēijī	airplane (M：**jià** 架）
船		chuán	boat，ship (M：**tiáo** 條）
葉	叶	yè	leaf (M：**piàn** 片）
紅葉	红叶	hóngyè	red leaves，fall foliage (M：**piàn** 片）
身體	身体	shēntǐ	body；health

Nínde shēntǐ zhēn búcuò.

您的身體真不錯。

(Physically, you are in
excellent shape.）

車站	车站	chēzhàn	station，terminal (M：**gè** 個）
火車站	火车站	huǒchēzhàn	railroad station
汽車站	汽车站	qìchēzhàn	bus stop，bus terminal
飛機場	飞机场	fēijīchǎng	airport (M：**gè** 個）
電影	电影	diànyǐng	movie (M：**gè** 個 for one film；**chǎng** 場 for a show）
電影院	电影院	diànyǐngyuàn	movie theater，cinema
電視	电视	diànshì	television (M：**jià** 架，**gè** 個）

ADVERBS（A）：

非常		fēicháng	unusually, extraordinarily

Zhè xīngqī rénrén dōu
fēicháng máng.

這星期人人都非常忙。

(This week everybody is
unusually busy.)

一定		yídìng	certainly, definitely

″Míngtiān wǒ qǐng nǐ chī
wǎnfàn, nǐ néng lái ba?″

″Wǒ yídìng lái.″

"明天我請你吃晚飯,你能來吧。"
"我一定來。"

(″I·ll invite you for dinner
tomorrow, will you come?″ ″Yes,
I certainly will.″)

一定得		yídìng děi (A/AV)	must; insist on

Yào shēntǐ jiànkāng, yídìng
děi cháng duànliàn.

要身體健康,一定得常鍛煉。

(To have good health, one must do
physical training constantly.)

多麼	多么	duōme	how, to what extent or degree (see note)

Nǐ xiǎng mǎi duōme dà de
fángzi?

你想買多麼大的房子。

(How large a house are you
thinking of buying?)

Měiguórén duōme ài xiǎoháizi a!

美國人多麼愛小孩子啊!

(Americans have an extraordinary
love for little children.)

這麼	这么	zhème	in this way, by this means, like this

Qǐng (nǐ) zhème zǒu.

請（你）這麽走。
(Please go this way.)

| 那麽 | 那么 | nàme | in that way, by that means, like that |

Wèishénme nǐ yào nàme zuò?

爲什麽你要那麽做？

(Why do you want to do it like that?)

| 怎麽 | 怎么 | zěnme | in what way? by what means? how? why? |

Nǐ zěnme hái bù zhǔnbèi gōngkè ne?

你怎麽還不準備功課呢？

(Why haven't you begun to do your homework?)

| 快（要）…了 | | kuài(yào)...le | soon, before long |

AUXILIARY VERB (AV):

| 應該 | 应该 | yīnggāi | have to, ought to |

Nǐ shì tā zuì hǎo de péngyou, nǐ yīnggāi zhīdao tāde yìsi.

你是她最好的朋友，你應該知道她的意思

(You are her best friend, you ought to know what she meant by that.)

COVERBS (CV): (see pattern and note)

| 從 | 从 | cóng | from (a place) |

Tā bùyídìng cóng nàr lái.

他不一定從那兒來。

[He won't necessarily come (here) from there.]

| 往 | | wǎng | toward (in a given direction) |

Nín yīnggāi cóng nàr wǎng

172

qián zǒu.

您應該從那兒往前走。

(You ought to go straight ahead
there.)

COVERBS/FUNCTIVE VERBS (CV/FV)：(see pattern and note)

到   dào   CV：to (a place as a destination)

FV：reach, arrive (a

place , see Lesson 9)

Tāmen hái méidào Niǔyuē qù ne.

他們還沒到紐約去呢。

(They haven't yet gone to New
York.)

來   来   lái   CV：to, for (introduces purpose
of action, see Lesson 9)

FV：come (here)

As CV：Tā lái jiāoshū (lái) ma?

她來教書（來）嗎？

(Is she coming to teach?)

As FV：Wǒ shì 1965 nián cóng
Rìběn lái Měiguó de.

我是1965年從日本來美國的。

(I came to the States from Japan
in 1965.)

去   qù   CV：to, for (gives purpose of action)

FV：go (there)

As CV：Wǒmen qù kàn diànyǐng
(qù)ba.

我們去看電影（去）吧。

(How about going to a movie?)

As FV：Tā dào xuéxiào qù jiàn
tā de lǎoshī qù le.

他到學校去見他的老師去了。

(He went to school to see his

173

		professor.)
坐	zuò	CV: by (a conveyance with a seat);
		FV: sit, ride on, ride in
		AS CV: Zuótiān tā zuò chuán dàole Shànghǎi.
		昨天她坐船到了上海。
		(She arrived in Shanghai by boat yesterday.)
		As FV: Qǐng zuò, hē yìdiǎnr chá.
		請坐，喝一點兒茶。
		(Please sit down and have some tea.)

FUNCTIVE VERBS (FV):

走	zǒu	walk, go; depart
		Jīntiān zǎoshang, tā zǒule.
		今天早上，他走了。
		(He left this morning.)
走走	zǒuzou	take a walk
		Wūzili tài chǎo, wǒmen dào wàitou qù zǒuzou ba.
		屋子裏太吵，我們到外頭去走走吧。
		(It's too noisy inside, let's go out to have a walk.)
開　开	kāi	drive (a car, engine); leave (of trains, boats, planes)
		Gōnggòng qìchē wǎng nǎr kāi?
		公共汽車往哪兒開？
		(Where does the bus leave for?)
		Kāi fēijī róngyì bùróngyì?
		開飛機容易不容易？
		(Is it easy to fly an airplane?)
飛　飞	fēi	fly
		Gāngcái nèi jià fēijī fēi le.

剛才那架飛機飛了。

(That airplane just took off a
second ago.)

| 騎 | 骑 | qí | ride on, ride in |

Nǐ huì qí zìxíngchē buhuì?

你會騎自行車不會？

(Can you ride a bicycle?)

| 考 | | kǎo | examine, take or give |
a test

Tiāntiān kǎo xuésheng de lǎoshī,
shì hǎo lǎoshī bushì?

天天考學生的老師，是好老師不是？

(Is the one who gives students
a test every day a good teacher?)

| 回 | | huí | return |

Shénme shíhou nǐ hé wǒ yìqǐ
huí xuéxiào?

什麼時候你和我一起回學校？

(When will you come back to
school with me?)

| 看見 | 看见 | kànjiàn | see (lit., look and perceive) |

Zuótiān wǎnshang wǒ kànjiàn
le yí wèi lǎo péngyou.

昨天晚上我看見了一位老朋友。

(Last night I saw an old friend
of mine.)

| 溫習 | 温习 | wēnxí | review |

Wēnxí gōngkè shì zuì méi
yìsi de shìqing.

溫習功課是最沒意思的事情。

(To review schoolwork is one of
the most boring things.)

| 鍛煉 | 锻炼 | duànliàn | do physical training, do |
physical fitness

Nǐ měitiān shénme shíhou

duànliàn?

你每天什麼時候鍛煉？

(When do you do your daily
physical fitness?)

| 準備 | 准备 | zhǔnbèi AV/FV) | prepare, get ready for, prepare to |

As AV： Wǒ zhǔnbèi míngnián
Liùyuè qù Zhōngguó.

我準備明年六月去中國。

(I'm planning to go to
China next June.)

As FV： Xiàxīngqī kǎoshì,
xiànzài wǒ bùnéng
bu zhǔnbèi gōngkè.

下星期考試，現在我不能不
準備功課。

(I'll have an examination
next week, so I cannot but
prepare it now.)

| 祝 | | zhù | wish |

STATIVE VERBS (SV)：

| 親愛 | 亲爱 | qīn·ài | dear；be intimate, be close |
| 錯 | 错 | cuò | be wrong, mistake |

Tāde shuōfa cuòle, tā bù
zhīdao zhèr de qíngkuàng.

她的説法錯了，她不知道這兒的情況

(What she says is wrong. She
doesn't understand the situation
here.)

Zhèr de huǒchē zhēn búcuò,
hěn piányi, yě hěn shūfu.

這兒的火車真不錯，很便宜，
也很舒服。

(The train ride here is really not bad, it is inexpensive but comfortable.)

健康		jiànkāng	(physically) healthy

Zhù nín jiànkāng.

祝您健康。

(I wish you good health.)

快樂	快乐	kuàilè (SV/N)	be happy, joyful; happiness

Tā lǎo shì fēicháng kuàilè.

她老是非常快樂。

(She is always very happy.)

VERB-OBJECTS (VO):

回家		huí jiā	return home

Jīnnián wǒ bùnéng huí jiā guònián.

今年我不能回家過年。

(This year I was not able to return home to celebrate the New Year.)

過節	过节	guò jié	celebrate a festival
上學	上学	shàng xué	attend school, go to school
回信		huí xìn	reply to a letter

Wǒ ài kàn xìn, kěnshì bú ài xiě huíxìn.

我愛看信,可是不愛寫回信。

(I love to read letters, but I don't like to answer them.)

考試	考试	kǎoshì (VO/N)	take or give an examination; examination, test

Xuésheng dōu búài kǎoshì, lǎoshī ài kǎoshì ma?

學生都不愛考試,老師愛考試嗎?

(None of the students like to take examinations. Do the teachers like to give exams?)

PROPER NAMES：

感恩節	感恩节	Gǎn·ēn Jié	Thanksgiving
聖誕節	圣诞节	Shèngdàn Jié	Christmas(in both PRC and Taiwan)
耶誕節	耶诞节	Yēdàn Jié	Christmas (In Hong Kong)
新年		Xīn Nián	New Year

EXPRESSIONS (EX)：

家書抵萬金		″Jiāshū dǐ	″One message from home is
	家书抵万金	wàn jīn″	worth a ton of gold.″ A line
			from the poem，″ A Spring View,″
			written by Du Fu of the Tang Dynasty
			(see note).
真不錯	真不错	zhēnbúcuò	not bad at all

PART III.　A LIST OF CHARACTERS REQUIRED TO BE REPRODUCED FROM MEMORY

火 車 汽 自 行 公 飛 機 船 信 身 體 封 條 非 定
應 該 往 去 坐 快 溫 準 備 走 騎 考 試 過 電 站
錯 場

PART IV.　SENTENCE PATTERNS

10.1. <u>The Movement of Sentence Subject</u>： The functive verb **lái** 來 indicates the subject is moving toward the speaker，while the functive verb **qù** 去 shows that the subject is moving away from the speaker. Both **lái** 來 and **qù** 去 are intransitive verbs. Usually, they cannot take any nouns as their subject, but they may be followed by place words to show destinations, such as:

Pattern: S FV.

or,   S lái/qù.

Ex 1: Tā **Lái** Měiguó le.

她來美國了。

(She has come to the United States.)

Ex 2: Wǒ kuàiyào **qù** tā nàr le.

我快要去他那兒了。

(I am going to his place soon.)

10.2. Coverb **Cóng** 從 for Starting Point: The coverb **cóng** 從 (from) is the most common coverb in Chinese to point out the place of origin.

Pattern: S (A) (AV) CV-PW lái/qù.

Ex 1: Wǒmen **cóng** xuéxiào lái.

我們從學校來。

(We come here from school.)

10.3. The Coverb **Dào** 到 Indicates the Destination of the Motion: In addition to the functive verbs **lái** and **qù**, a popular structure using the coverb **dào** can also take place-words as its objects to show the destination of the journey.

Pattern: S (A) (AV) dào-PW lái/qù.

Ex 1: Nǐ fùqīn **dào** Táiwān qù le ma?

你父親到臺灣去了嗎?

(Did your father go to Taiwan?)

Ex 2: Wǒ mèimei míngtiān **dào** wǒ zhèr **lái.**

我妹妹明天到我這兒來。

(My younger sister will come here to my place tomorrow.)

10.4. How to Show Starting Point and Destination in a Single Sentence: As a rule, the starting point is always placed before the destination in a sentence:

A.   With the Coverbs **Cóng** 從 and **Dào** 到:

Pattern: S (A) (AV) cóng-starting point dào-destination lái/qù.

Ex 1: Tā zhǔnbèi **cóng** Fǎguó **dào** Táiběi **qù.**

他準備從法國到臺北去。

(He plans to go to Taipei from France.)

Ex 2: Tā bù néng **cóng** fēijīchǎng **dào** wǒ jiā **lai**.

他不能從飛機場到我家來。

(He can't come to my house from the airport.)

B.   Without the Coverb **Dào** 到:

Pattern: S (A) (AV) **cóng**-starting point **lái/qù** destination.

Ex 1: Hěnduō xuésheng **cóng** Měiguó **qù** Zhōngguó le.

很多學生從美國去中國了。

(There were many students who went to China from the United States.)

Ex 2: Xiàle kè, wǒ yào **cóng** xuéxiào **qù** huǒchēzhàn.

下了課，我要從學校去火車站。

(When the class is over, I'll go to the railroad station from the school.)

10.5.   The Coverb **Zuò** 坐 Indicates the Means of Conveyance: In order to indicate the means of conveyance used in coming or going, the coverb **zuò** 坐 (moving by sitting) is the most common. The object of the coverb **zuò** 坐 is not a place word. In fact, it refers to the subject's mode of transportation. Furthermore, the coverb **zuò** 坐 can be replaced by other verbs which indicate the manner of operating the conveyance, such as **qí** 騎 for riding on a bicycle or a horse, and **kāi** 開 as operating a car, a plane or a boat, etc.

Pattern: S (A) (AV) **zuò**-means of conveyance **lái/qù**.

Ex 1: Wǒmen kěyǐ **qí** zìxíngchē dào zhèr **lái**.

我們可以騎自行車到這兒來。

(We can come here by riding bicycles.)

Ex 2: Nǐmen **zuò** shénme chē dào nàr **qù**?

你們坐什麼車到那兒去？

(What kind of transportation are you taking to go there?)

Besides example #2, inquiry concerning means of conveyance can be made with two clauses, such as: **Nǐ dào nàr qù, zěnme qù?** 你到那兒去，怎麼去？(What kind of transportation are you taking to go there?)

10.6.   The Coverb **wǎng** 往 for Direction: The coverb **wǎng** 往 is used to show the direction toward which the subject moves. The object of this coverb must be a noun indicating direction so it can be called a directional noun. Three structures are involved here:

A.   The expression **wǎng**-directional noun provides information concerning direction of motion, and it modifies the main verb **lái** 來 or **qù** 去:

180

Pattern: S (A) (AV) **wǎng**-dir. noun **lái/qù.**

Ex 1: Wǒ bú yào **wǎng** zuǒbiānr **qù.**

我不要往左邊兒去。

(I'm not going to the left.)

B.　The functive verbs used in this construction are other than **lái** 來 or **qù** 去, to express the kind of action performed by the subject as it moves toward the indicated direction.

Pattern: S (A) (AV) **wǎng**-dir. noun FV.

Ex 1: Qìchē **wǎng** qiántou kāi le.

汽車往前頭開了.

(The car runs straight forward.)

Ex 2: Qǐng **wǎng** qián zǒu.

請往前走。

(Please move straight ahead.)

C.　The construction "**wǎng xià**" has two usages:

1. **Wǎng xià** 往下 indicates that the action is progressing downward when the functive verb intrinsically embodies a physical movement from one place to another.

Pattern: S (A) (AV) **wǎng-xià** (tou) FV.

Ex: Bié **wǎng** xià zǒu.

別往下走。

(Don't go down.)

2. **Wǎng xià** 往下 means "continuing the action", if the functive verb indicates an action that does not require physical movement from one place to another.

Pattern: O, S (A) (AV) **wǎng—xià** FV.

Ex 1: Shū, qǐng nǐ **wǎng xià** niàn.

書,請你往下念。

(Please continue to read aloud.)

Ex 2: Xìn, wǒ búyuànyi **wǎng xià** xiě le.

信,我不願意往下寫了。

(I don't want to continue writing the letter.)

10.7.　Use Coverb **Lái** 來 or **Qù** 去 to Introduce the Purpose of Actions:　**Lái** 來 or **Qù** 去 indicates the purpose of an action. In this capacity, they can be interpreted as "to" or "for." The objects of the coverbs can be place words, or they can appear in the form

181

of "Verb-Object. "

Pattern: S (A) (AV) CV-O lái/qù.

    Ex 1: Xiànzài wǒ yīnggāi qù shàngkè qù.

        現在我應該去上課去。

        (Now I have to go to class.)

    Ex 2: Zhāng jiàoshòu děi dào Bōshìdùn lái zuò fēijī lái.

        張教授得到波士頓來坐飛機來。

        (Prof. Zhang has to come to Boston in order to catch an airplane.)

In each sentence, the word lái 來 or qù 去 appears twice. Semantically, however, they are not identical. The difference is due to the syntax. Obviously, the first lái 來 or qù 去 is a coverb meaning "to " or "for "and the second one is a functive verb meaning "come" or "go. " Because of these characteristics a sentence contains a coverbial phrase introducing the purpose of action, which may appear in these forms in a simple sentence:

A.   A complete sentence may include both the coverb and the functive verb:

Pattern: S (A) (AV) lái/qù-VO lái/qù.

    Ex 1: Míngtiān wǒ péngyou xiǎngyào lái kàn nǐmen lái.

        明天我朋友想要來看你們來。

        (My friend wants to come to visit you tomorrow.)

    Ex 2: Gāngcái tā qù túshūguǎn qù le.

        剛才她去圖書館去了。

        (Just now she went to the library.)

B. An "incomplete sentence" may omit either the coverb or the functive verb and still retain the meaning of the sentence.

    1. Without coverb:

Pattern: S (A) (AV) VO lái/qù.

    Ex 1: Míngtiān wǒ péngyou xiǎngyào kàn nǐmen lái.

        明天我朋友想要看你們來。

        (My friend wants to come to visit you tomorrow.)

    Ex 2: Gāngcái tā qù túshūguǎn kànshū qù le.

        剛才她去圖書館看書去了。

        (Just now she went to the library to study.)

    2. Without functive verb:

Pattern: S (A) (AV) lái/qù VO.

Ex 1：Míngtiān wǒ péngyou xiǎngyào **lái** kàn nǐmen.

明天我朋友想要來看你們。

(My friend wants to come to visit you tomorrow.)

Ex 2：Gāngcái tā qù túshūguǎn qù kàn shū le.

剛才她去圖書館去看書了。

(Just now she went to the library to study.)

10.8. **All Coverbial Phrases Pertaining to Movement are Parallel Phrases**： A sentence indicating movement may contain two or more coverbial phrases, therefore, the proper word order must be observed. Neither **dào** 到 nor **lái** 來 or **qù** 去 can be used as the first coverbial phrase in a series of parallel phrases. The possible arrangements of parallel phrases are as follows：

A. Sentences showing only starting point and destination：

Pattern 1：S (A) (AV) **cóng**-PW1 **dào** PW2 **lái/qù.**

Ex：Wǒ yào **cóng** sùshè **dào** jiàoshì **qù.**

我要從宿舍到教室去。

(I am going to the classroom from the dormitory.) or,

Pattern 2：S (A) (AV) **cóng**-PW1 **lái/qù** PW2.

Ex：Wǒ yào cóng sùshè qù jiàoshì.

我要從宿舍去教室。

(I am going to the classroom from the dormitory.)

B. Adding coverbial phrase indicating means of action：

Pattern 1：S (A) (AV) **cóng**-PW1 **zuò**-m. of conv. **láiqù** PW2.

Pattern 2：S (A) (AV) **cóng**-PW1 **zuò**-m. of conv. **dào**-PW2 **lái/qù.**

Ex：Shéi dōu bùnéng cóng Fǎguó zuò huǒchē lái Měiguó?

誰都不能從法國坐火車來美國。

(Nobody can come to the United States from France by train.)

Note, the positions of **cóng**-PW1 and **zuò**-means of conveyance in the above mentioned patterns are interchangeable.

C. Adding coverbial phrases indicating the purpose of action：

Pattern：S (A) (AV) **cóng**-PW1 **zuò**-m. of conv. **dào**-PW2 **lái/qù** VO **lái/qù.**

Ex：Wǒ jiějie cóng Xiānggǎng zuò fēijī **dào** Měiguó **lái** kàn tā nǚér **lái** le.

我姐姐從香港坐飛機到美國來看她女兒來了。

(My sister came by airplane to the States from Hong Kong to visit her daughter.)

D.　Adding coverbial phrase specifying direction:

Pattern: S (A) (AV) **cóng**-PW1 zuò-m. of conv. **wăng**-dir. (FV) **dào**-PW2 **lái/**
qù.

Ex: Tā **cóng** chénglitou kāi qìchē **wăng** dōng (kāi)**dào** fēijīchǎng **qù** le.

他從城裏頭開汽車往東（開）到飛機場去了。

(He drove a car from the city eastward to the airport.)

10.9.　<u>Using Coverbial Expressions Pertaining to Movement to Modify Nouns</u>:　Since the coverbial phrases for location and existence can be used as modifiers of nouns, the same applies to the coverbial phrases pertaining to movement. To use the coverbial expressions, just follow the same pattern as indicated in Lesson 9:

Pattern: **CV-O FV de N**

Ex 1: cóng Měiguó lái **de** kèrén

從美國來的客人

(the guest who comes from the States)

Ex 2: lái shàng kè **de** xuésheng

來上課的學生

(the student who comes to class)

Ex 3: zuò huǒchē zǒu **de** péngyou

坐火車走的朋友

(the friend who left by train)

Ex 4: dào fàndiàn chīfàn qù **de** rén

到飯店吃飯去的人

(the one who goes to the restaurant to eat)

Ex 5: wăng qián fēi **de** fēijī

往前飛的飛機

(the airplane that flies straight ahead)

PART V.　GRAMMAR NOTES AND OTHERS

1.　Coverbs cannot take the verb suffix le 了 to express completion of action. Thus, in order to present a sentence in the past tense, you must place the particle **le** 了 after the functive verb **lái** 來 or **qù** 去 or other main verbs in the sentence, as in **Wǒ zuótiān zǎoshang cóng shítáng dào jiàoshì qù shàngkè qù le.** 我昨天早上從食堂到教室去上課去了。(Yesterday morning I went to the classroom from the cafeteria to attend class.) Even in an incomplete sentence with the omission of the main verb **lái** 來 or **qù** 去, you still have to place the particle **le** 了 at the end of the sentence--not after the coverb **lái** 來 or **qù** 去 --to indicate the completion of action.

> Ex 1: **Jīntiān zhōngwǔ wǒ dào chéngwàitou qù wánr le.**
>
> 今天中午我到城外頭去玩兒了。
>
> (At noon time today, I went outside of the city to play.)
>
> Ex 2: **Tā cóng Běijīng lái shàngxué le.**
>
> 他從北京來上學了。
>
> (She came from Beijing to attend school.)

2. Even though coverbial phrases pertaining to movement are parallel phrases that can be put into the same sentence, the coverbial phrase **zài** 在 -PW cannot be treated in the same way. This is because **zài** 在 does not refer to motion.

3. The coverbial phrase indicating purpose of action is the coverbial expression in the series of the parallel phrases. Hence, you can switch the position of the coverbial expression for means of action: **zuò** 坐 -means, with **cóng** 從-PW, but you cannot change its position with **dào** 到-PW. In other words, the expression of **zuò** 坐-means of conveyance must precede the expression of destination. Otherwise, it will indicate the purpose of action. This can be seen by comparing the following two sentences:

> (1) **Tā zuò chuán cóng zhèr dào Rìběn qù le.**
>
> 他坐船從這兒到日本去了。
>
> (He went to Japan from here by boat.)
>
> (2) **Tā cóng zhèr dào Rìběn qù zuò chuán (qù) le.**
>
> 他從這兒到日本去坐船（去）了。
>
> (He went to Japan from here to get on board.)

4. For the purpose of emphasis or contrast, a coverbial phrase may assume the topic position. In such cases, **lái** 來 or **qù** 去 are usually repeated after the main verb, as for example: **Dào Zhōngguó qù, zuò fēijī qù hǎo** 到中國去，坐飛機去好 (In going to China, it's best to go by plane.) or **Dào zhèr lái, zuò chuán lái piányi yìdiǎnr** 到這兒來，坐船來便宜一點兒 (In coming here, it's cheaper to come by boat.)

5. The Full Text of the Poem "Chūn Wàng 春望" (*A Spring View*):

Guó pò shān hé zài, chéng chūn cǎo mù shēn.

Gǎn shí huā jiàn lèi, hèn bié niǎo jīng xīn.

Fēnghuǒ lián sānyuè, jiāshū dǐ wànjīn.

Bái tóu sāo gèng duǎn, hún yù bú shèng zān.

English Translation:

Though a country be sundered, hills and rivers endure;

And spring comes green again to trees and grasses,

Where petals have been shed like tears,

And lonely birds have sung their grief.

... After the war-fires of three months,

One message from home is worth a ton of gold.

... I stroke my white hair. It has grown too thin

To hold the hairpins anymore.

國破山河在,城春草木深。

感時花濺泪,恨別鳥驚心。

烽火連三月,家書抵萬金。

白頭搔更短,渾欲不勝簪。

6. The suggested reading in *Essential Grammar for Modern Chinese* is: Chapter IV——Classification of Sentences (1) The Mood, pp. 48-54; and Chapter XIV——Coverb (3), Pertaining to Movement.

PART VI.   TRANSLATION OF THE TEXT

A Letter Home

One Saturday afternoon in November, after lunch Gao Gui didn't want to go out, nor did he want to prepare his school assignments in the library. His fellow classmates had all gone out to enjoy themselves. He realized it would soon be Thanksgiving. He wouldn't be able to join his family at home this year. He was terribly homesick, and wanted very much to have the turkey his mother would cook. He thought he ought to write a letter and tell his parents about his life as a student in China.

He wrote the following:

November 5 , 1983

Dear Dad and Mom:

How have you been? I've received Mom's letter of October 28 today. The happiest event for a person living abroad is to receive letters from home. Now I can truly understand the meaning of "a letter from home is worth a ton of gold."

My schoolmates and I rode our bicycles to the Fragrant Hills last month. I saw the fall foliage there. It must also be the most beautiful season of the year in Wellesley. How I wish I could get on the airplane and fly back home to visit you, and spend the Thanksgiving holiday at home. But soon I will have examinations. I must stay here at school to review my lessons.

My living and learning situation here is quite nice. However, I feel quite exhausted because of the busy schedule. Every morning before breakfast I do physical exercises. Then I ride my bike to school. I have lunch at the school cafeteria. The food is not bad at all. After school is over in the afternoon, I take a walk on the streets. After dinner, I usually prepare homework in the dormitory. I often go to see movies at the theater just next to my school. I also watch television sometimes. I don't like to go to the library, because it is usually very crowded and it is hard to find a seat. Now I often chat with my Chinese friends.

187

Sometimes I even tell stories in Chinese.

During the New Year holidays, some schoolmates and I are planning to take the train from Beijing to Shanghai. From there, we'll go to Hong Kong by boat for one week of vacation. I'll write to you again when I return to Beijing.

Best wishes for health and happiness.

Your loving son
Gao Gui

漢語初階（上）

Helen T. Lin

*

©華語教學出版社

華語教學出版社出版

（中國北京百萬莊路 24 號）

郵政編碼 100037

北京外文印刷廠印刷

中國國際圖書貿易總公司發行

（中國北京車公莊西路 35 號）

北京郵政信箱第 399 號　郵政編碼 100044

1992 年（16 開）第一版

1996 年第二次印刷

（漢英）

ISBN 7－8005　　　・106（外）

46.00

9－CE－2406PA